DUST OF THE D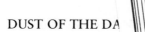

Ian Mathie spent his childhood and
Africa. After a short service commission in the RAF, he
returned to the continent as a rural development officer
working for the British government and a number of other
agencies. His work in water resources and related projects
during the 1970s brought him into close contact with the
African people, their cultures and varied tribal customs,
many of which are now all but lost. These experiences,
recorded in his notebooks, were the inspiration for a series
of African memoirs, of which *Dust of the Danakil* is the
fourth volume. Ian continued to visit Africa until health
considerations curtailed his travelling. He now lives in
south Warwickshire with his wife and dog.

By the same author

Other titles in the African Memoir Series:
BRIDE PRICE
MAN IN A MUD HUT
SUPPER WITH THE PRESIDENT
THE MAN OF PASSAGE

KEEP TAKING THE PILLS

DUST OF THE DANAKIL

*For Gill & Phil,
with love & best wishes*

Ian Mathie

Ian Mathie

MOSAÏQUEPRESS

First published in the UK in 2012 by
MOSAÏQUE PRESS
Registered office:
70 Priory Road
Kenilworth, Warwickshire CV8 1LQ
www.mosaïquepress.co.uk

Cover design by Gary Henderson
GH Graphic Design Ltd

Printed in the UK.

ISBN 978-1-906852-13-9

To the memory of Ali Waré,
who might never have become such a good friend
if his proficiency with a shovel had been better

and to all my other friends among the
Dodha and Abu Sama'ara Afar tribes.

List of maps

Contents

Author's note

THE PLACES, PEOPLE AND incidents described in this story are true. The names of two individuals mentioned in the text have been changed at their request to respect their privacy. The names of all the others are those by which I knew them.

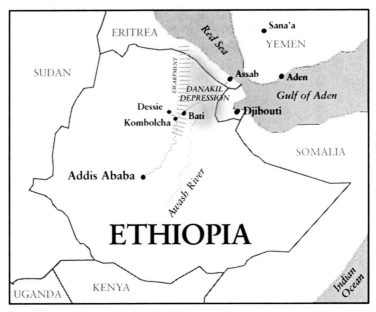

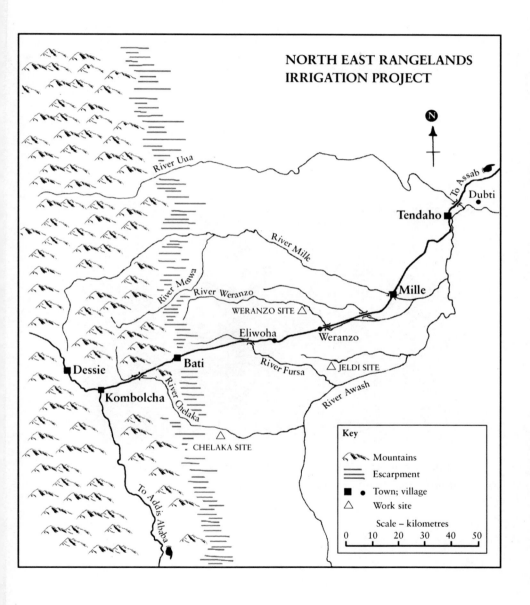

**NORTH EAST RANGELANDS
IRRIGATION PROJECT**

N

River Uua

To Assab

Dubti

Tendaho

River Mille

River Mawa

River Weranzo

WERANZO SITE

Mille

Eliwoha

Weranzo

Dessie

Bati

River Fursa

JELDI SITE

Kombolcha

River Chelaka

River Awash

CHELAKA SITE

To Addis Ababa

Key

Mountains

Escarpment

■ • Town; village

△ Work site

Scale – kilometres

0   10   20   30   40   50

Some of our Afar 'greeting party' mourning a tribesman in the months following our arrival in the Danakil.

1 ~ Reconnaissance

NIGHT COMES QUICKLY in the desert. We stopped a few miles from the road to make camp and feed ourselves as soon as the sun went down. There was no point in continuing our search for the Afar at night if they hadn't allowed us to make contact by day. After supper, three of us stretched out on camp beds but Elamu, our driver, and Dagu, the interpreter, elected to roll out their blankets on the roof rack atop the Land Rover.

Some time around 3am, I was awoken by Dagu, his finger over my mouth in warning. He pointed into the darkness, raised five fingers in front of my face and pulled an imaginary trigger: there were five men out there armed with guns. I looked quickly in the direction he pointed. I could see nothing but was aware of a distinct and not-yet-familiar aroma wafting in on the soft night breeze. It was strong, smelled like over-ripe blue cheese and seemed a most incongruous scent to encounter in the Ethiopian desert. It could only mean one thing: the people we had not seen before were here now and had chosen this moment to surprise us.

"They are moving slowly but will be here in less than ten minutes," Dagu said in a whisper. I put my head close to his.

"Wake the others," I whispered back, "tell them to lie under the Land Rover and keep quiet."

Then I took my heavy torch and sneaked off into the bush in the opposite direction without using the light. About a hundred yards out I turned left and began moving in a wide arc that should take me behind our visitors before they came too close to our camp. It was hazardous going, weaving my way between the camel thorn bushes. They were savage, and each time I snagged an arm or leg on them I had to bite my lip hard to keep from making any sound.

Eight minutes after I left our camp, I saw the men I was stalking. They were in a small group to my left. I froze and held my breath. Their white *ga'abis* stood out in the waning moonlight and made them easy to see. Two of the men appeared to have rifles. The other three carried spears. All had large knives called *gillés* strapped across their waists. They were moving cautiously, as if wary of making an attack like this at night, uncertain how the people they were approaching might react.

From their position, our camp was clearly in sight. They had to be able to see our two tents with the Land Rover parked between them. The light was too weak for me to see any detail in the camp so I was unsure whether the other members of our team were safely under the vehicle. But there was no time left to speculate. The visitors were getting ready to make their move.

I moved in closer to them, carefully. A twig snapping underfoot would betray my presence. The men were now only twenty yards from our camp. They stopped and muttered quietly to one another, clearly deciding their tactics. I moved closer.

As one of them raised his rifle to his shoulder, I stepped up close behind him and snatched it from his hands, tossing it backwards over my shoulder and hoping that the jolt when it landed would not fire the weapon. At the same moment I used the few words of Afar I had learned. "Hello and welcome to our camp!" I said as I turned the torch on with my other hand and stepped back.

The man with the other rifle swung towards me so I shone the torch in his eyes, side-stepped and, reaching out from the darkness, took hold of the rifle and pulled it sharply from his grasp.

Someone in our camp chose that moment to turn on the Land Rover's headlights, illuminating the whole scene and destroying the cover that the darkness had given me. I made a show of throwing the second rifle away, over my shoulder, and made gestures for the five tribesmen to sit. They hesitated, uncertain, and then squatted as I called for Dagu to come forward so that we could talk to them.

I squatted to be on the same level as them and asked, "Why have you come here with guns, like thieves in the night?"

"We do not know you. We must be careful," one of the men said. "We are not thieves."

"Then why not make noise to announce your arrival?"

"We were afraid," the man replied. "We do not know you or why you have come here."

"There is nothing to be afraid of," I said. "Come and drink tea with us. We'll tell you why we have come." I offered my hand to the nearest man and stood up, lifting him with me as he grasped it tentatively. After a moment's hesitation the others followed, still looking wary. Dagu was talking rapidly, trying to reassure them.

As we moved towards our camp I could see the other members of our team scrambling out from under the Land Rover. "Someone make tea," I called out. However they had come to us, these were the people we needed to engage.

Our visitors declined the chairs we offered, preferring to squat and sit on their heels. Over the next few weeks I came to recognise this posture as one used for talking and to adopt it myself whenever we negotiated with these tribesmen, which was often.

Speaking through Dagu, I introduced our party and told them we were water specialists who had come here to the Danakil desert because of the drought. We asked their names and learned that they were called Digeye, Ali Mbei, Farasabba Dou, Adune and Jumai. Digeye, who appeared to be the oldest, acted as their spokesman, reaching out to touch each man on his arm as he named him.

In a few minutes Elamu brought the kettle of tea. He placed it on the ground next to me and gave me seven empty food cans. So, I thought to myself, that's why he hadn't crushed them after meals and put them in the sack with the rest of our rubbish. I poured tea into the tins and passed them round. Elamu had told me when he put the kettle down that it was sweet and I realised he knew a lot of things I had yet to learn. The tea obviously met with the Afars' approval for they sucked at it noisily and muttered to one another in approving tones. Dagu confirmed they liked the sweetness. I poured a tin for him and took a small one myself. I had developed many African tastes in my years working there, but sweet tea was not one of them.

We talked until the pre-dawn calm allowed the dust to settle round our small encampment and the eastern horizon became visible, a thin grey line in the blackness. As dawn approached, we got our first clear look at the men who had sneaked up on us in the night.

They were slim men, about five foot eight tall, with dark skins and fine, clean-shaven features. Their dark eyes were alert and watchful and their hands showed strength while bearing no calluses to suggest they had experienced hard work.

Each was dressed in a soft white cotton cloth, draped over his shoulders like a cloak, with a second, similar cloth around his waist like a kilt. All wore crude sandals made from untanned goat skin, with wide soles and broad straps to hold them on their feet. As well as their large daggers, three of the men carried five foot spears, with a narrow head and a strip of iron wound in a spiral round its heel. We would become familiar with both the daggers and spears in the months to come.

The men's hair was naturally black and loosely curled, now coated with a fine layer of desert dust which had stuck to the pungent smelling grease with which they had earlier dressed it. Farasabba Dou and Jumai had theirs shaped like winged crowns but the others wore their hair cut shorter and not so distinctive.

Standing, they had upright postures and they moved with a fluid grace. To sit they simply bent their knees and sank, upright, onto their heels into a posture they could maintain for hours but from which they could rise rapidly should the need arise.

When it was fully light, I walked into the desert and retrieved their rifles, checking each one for load and safety as I brought them back. One of the weapons was a rusty Belgian rifle dating from the First World War with just three rounds in the magazine. The other was Russian and so old it could have dated from the Crimean War. The engraving in Cyrillic script on its stock said 'Sebastapol 1854', suggesting it had been used at the siege. It had five rounds in the clip but it was clear they were unlikely to go off; by the marks on their percussion caps, they had all previously been struck by a firing pin, as had the rounds in the Belgian rifle. I was to discover this was common among the weapons of the

Afar. For them, a rifle was an important status symbol; possession of one was enhanced by the number of cartridges the owner carried in his bandolier. The condition of the rounds or whether they could be fired from his rifle didn't seem to matter. Any anxiety I might previously have felt about being among these gun-toting tribesmen was significantly reduced by this discovery.

Walking back to the group, I pulled my shirt tail out of my waistband and used it to wipe the worst of the dust off the weapons before handing them back to their owners, who received them with a nod of recognition and remained squatting where they were.

THE SUN CAME UP in a burst of glory and within moments the air temperature was rising. The breeze, which had died in the half hour before dawn, resumed and small swirls of dust skittered across the grey countryside, dancing between the thorn bushes.

I was hungry but it was clear we couldn't eat in front of these men without offering them a share of our food. I said to Dagu, "Will you ask these men when they last had food?"

There was a brief discussion before he said, "Four days ago they had some goat milk."

"Tell them we have bread and more tea. We would be pleased if they will share it with us." I watched the men's faces closely as Dagu repeated this. Deep hunger overcame their natural reserve and it was clear from their reactions that they accepted. Elamu wasted no time in getting the kettle boiling again and the tea tins were soon refilled. We divided two large loaves and shared these out among our visitors, keeping small portions for ourselves.

The man who had identified himself as Digeye asked why we were eating so little. We explained that we had eaten the previous day and were not as hungry as him and his friends, so we didn't need food as much. They should eat the bread as they might not have food later. This prompted further enquiries about why we had come to the Danakil and we went through the whole thing again, explaining that news had reached people beyond the desert that the Afar were suffering from the drought and that they needed food, so we had been sent to look into the possibility of helping them grow food.

"You can't grow food here," Digeye responded. "The only things that grow are thorns and sticks. Even the grass has given up growing."

"When did it last rain here?" I asked.

"I have never seen rain," he told me.

I looked at him carefully and estimated that he must be somewhere between thirty-five and forty years old. If he had never seen rain, this desert had been a long time dry.

"When I was a boy my grandfather told me he had seen rain," one of the others said. "It made the land turn green." He appeared to be a few years younger than Digeye and I guessed this meant he was talking about a period more than forty years earlier.

During subsequent discussion with the Afar, we discovered that there had been no significant rain in the region for longer than that. The few showers that were reported had been localised and brief, and had done no more than enable the tiny *tribulus* plants to bloom. Those showers had not been enough to support new grass or shrub growth. The few plants that persisted in this desert hung onto life because they could capture the minimal humidity of the night air through their leaves or because they had very deep root systems able to access underground aquifers well beyond the depth to which the local people could dig wells.

AS WE TALKED, WE explained about the plan that had brought us to their homeland, to capture water coming down the dry *wadis* from the mountains and spread it on the land. We described the sort of locations we were looking for and asked our guests if they knew any areas that matched our descriptions. For ten minutes or so they argued among themselves and then suggested there were three places within a few hours walk of where we were sitting. There was no point in packing up camp just to see these, so we decided to leave the camp as it was, split our party and leave one man and our driver here with three of the Afar, while the other two took the Land Rover with the interpreter and the two remaining Afar to have a look the places they told us about.

Since I was the only one who could use a sextant and thus establish precise locations for the sites, I was to be one of the two who went. The other was our irrigation engineer, Bruce, whose job was to produce the preliminary designs for any system that I was going to stay and build. Dr Abel, the third member of our team, elected to remain behind and rest.

The two Afar chosen to come with us were Digeye and Farasabba Dou. They appeared at first to be leading us on a rather circuitous route, but it soon became apparent that they knew what they were doing. Every time we came to one of the numerous *wadis* that stretched across the desert, they unfailingly delivered us to a point where the banks had crumbled, giving easy passage for the vehicle. These *wadis* were great gashes in the land, often deeper than ten feet, and had we tried to cross elsewhere it would have been impossible without digging ramps. The points our guides chose had been worn down by the regular passage of livestock on their way to or from grazing lands beyond.

We looked at two sites that day. Neither was ideal, but one

could be used if we could find nothing better. When we returned to our camp just before sunset, we found Dr Abel and Elamu very pleased to see us. They had spent a nervous day in the company of three armed Afar men with whom they could not communicate and most certainly didn't trust.

Dr Abel was a twitchy individual. His role in the team was far from clear. He was some sort of a boffin, more accustomed to the dry corridors of academe than the arid openness of a real desert under drought conditions. As I understood it, he had been imposed on our mission at the last minute by the mandarins in London, and he obviously didn't like being here. He could see no redeeming features in the unusual tribesmen our mission was designed to help and made no secret of the fact that he hated camping. These things made me wonder what sort of a hold London had over him to oblige him to join the mission. Maybe it was purely mercenary and they were paying him a fat fee. If so, what for? I never did find out.

By contrast, Bruce was an ideal companion on a trip like this. Calm and unflappable, he had worked in deserts before. He understood terrain, knew what sort of ground we should be looking for and was able to explain complex irrigation principles in simple terms that made sense to those with no knowledge. He was also easy to get along with, adaptable and capable.

While we had been out this first day, he had taught me how to use the surveying instruments he had brought with him to assess the general slope and direction of the land we were exploring. The land may have looked flat but, as I discovered, the eye is easily deceived. In return I had taught him to use the sextant and tables to fix our position.

Over supper that evening, we decided that I would remain in

camp the next day and Bruce would take Dr Abel and Elamu with him to look at the third site our new Afar friends had told us about. It would take a whole day to go and explore the one location, which was much further north, up near the Uua River.

River was a bit of a misnomer. It had carried no water for at least ten years, but was a significant channel carved across the desert and the Afar said there were a number of places along its length where water could be found within a few feet of the surface for most of the year. It was also surrounded by large areas of flat grazing land where once the tribes had maintained large herds of long-horned cattle.

The mention of tribes got me wondering, so I asked the names of the tribes to which the three places they were showing us belonged. They told us they were all within the traditional territory of their own Dodha tribe. Their answer made me ask about the tribes themselves, how many there were, where each one had its homelands and what the tribal structure was. There was not time to pursue immediately all the enquiries I wanted to make but I resolved to use the day after the trip to Uua River, while the other two were drawing up diagrams of possible irrigation systems and drafting preliminary reports, to use Dagu and ask more. That would be useful groundwork for what I would have to do later.

THE GROUP SET OFF at dawn the next morning, leaving me in camp with Ali Mbei, Farasabba Dou and Jumai. Adune had gone with the party this time as he was more familiar with that area than the others, having grazed his herd there each spring for the last three years.

After they left I put the kettle on, made more tea and set about acquiring some new Afar words. To start, this was a crude process involving holding up objects and asking what they were called. My companions soon got the idea and joined in enthusiastically, naming everything around the encampment that had any relevance to them. I noticed that they either ignored technical items or gave them names that sounded as if they had been derived from Italian or French. It was only then that I remembered that nearby Djibouti was a French territory, commonly referred to as the *Territoire Français des Afars et des Issas*, or TFAI.

"*On parle français?*" I tried in case any of these men had been there and learned some of that language.

Farasabba Dou's eyes lit up. "*Oui, un peu,*" he responded. He didn't know a lot, but it was enough to give us a little common ground. From then on my language lesson made great progress. The hours flew by and before I realised how late it was, the sun was going down and I was wondering where the others had got to. They should have been back by now.

I prepared food, cooking a large pot of rice and adding some rather tired looking vegetables we had brought down from the mountains with us. My Afar companions watched with interest. I asked them to name each ingredient as I put them together, making notes as I did so in order to be able to revise and remember them later.

When the rice was cooked, the four of us shared a large bowl, together with some flat bread, baked under the cooking fire. We set a share aside for the others to eat when they got back.

These men, who had seemed slightly tentative to begin with, had relaxed by now and watched everything I did with curiosity rather than the suspicion that had been obvious to start with. In return, I had decided that they were no threat to me and the fact that they were all armed with fearsome knives had entirely slipped from my consciousness. I realised that I had also become accustomed to the smell of rancid butter that accompanied them. One man, Jumai, was particularly vain and kept looking at himself in a small piece of mirror that he kept in a little pocket at the back of his scabbard. He was constantly preening to make sure his hair looked just how he wanted it.

I observed later that it was particularly the younger men who dressed their hair in a winged crown, although even the older ones loved to apply the butter dressing. The observation prompted a memo in my notebook to buy a supply of small mirrors when we returned to the mountains; they could be a useful bargaining currency later, when we got round to negotiations about work.

The night wore on and the moon rose. Still the others were not back and I was growing concerned that something might have happened. I began to keep watch on the northern horizon, hoping to see the Land Rover's headlights as they wove their way back across the *wadis*, but the horizon remained dark. I strained my ears, listening for the sound of the engine, but the gentle sighing of the night breeze through the thorny branches of nearby bushes was enough to mask any more distant sounds. I wouldn't be able to hear the vehicle until it was quite close.

So we sat around our small camp fire, drinking yet more sweet tea and waiting, dozing and wondering why the others were delayed. After a time, the three Afar men lay down and slept while I continued to keep watch. Inevitably I dozed off, to be shaken awake by Ali Mbei who was pointing out into the bush and making gestures to indicate that someone was coming. I listened carefully but could hear nothing.

The breeze had dropped and the air was still. Sound should

have carried well but all I could hear was my own breathing and the slight clicking as small pieces of charcoal in the dying fire cooled and cracked. The moon was almost down now and only the bright starlight illuminated the bush. I could see my three companions well enough, but everything beyond a few yards away was in inky blackness. I found my torch and stood up to see if height would give me a better view, but could still see nothing.

Suddenly Ali Mbei was clutching at my arm, pointing out into the darkness with his other hand. I directed the torch where he indicated and switched it on, expecting to see someone walking towards us. Instead I saw five pairs of still red eyes and dark, shadowy bodies. Moments later they were all in motion as a volley of stones launched by Jumai and Farasabba Dou landed among them and the group scattered. There was a whooping cry and scuffling feet as all the eyes vanished from the pool of light cast by my torch. That sound, and the brief glimpse as their owners retreated from the light, told me this was a group of spotted hyenas out on the prowl. If we hadn't woken up, we could have been badly mauled. For all their reputation of being scavengers, these animals can be savage hunters; their jaws are more than capable of going through a man's leg. I didn't much fancy becoming dinner for a hungry hyena.

My three Afar companions started shouting and making as much noise as possible. Jumai picked up an empty cooking pot and started beating it with the handle of his spear. The racket would certainly be heard a long way off and I hoped it was enough to keep the hyenas at bay. We gathered sticks from the nearby bushes, built up our campfire and started another kettle of water heating for tea to sustain us through the rest of the night. We weren't going to get any more sleep after this.

The ground where we had camped was stony and the three Afar men soon collected another pile of missiles in case the hyenas came back. They had scattered in the same direction, but these were persistent animals and, unless they had eaten well in the last few days, were unlikely to take this first rebuff as anything serious. It was obvious the Afar understood them well. They were accustomed to defending their herds against night marauders and they were not going to be caught unawares again. Every few minutes one of them would stand up and launch a series of small rocks out into the darkness. On two occasions there were yelps as a missile found a target, followed by a brief scuffling as the animals ran off.

A while later we heard a shout and a whistle. I knew Elamu carried a whistle, so I shouted into the darkness. The answering shout was encouraging and I started waving my torch in that direction. Soon we could hear them clearly. They shouted that they could see our fire and a few minutes later a tired party stumbled into camp. They were all thirsty; their water had run out soon after darkness overtook them. After slaking their thirst, they fell upon the food we had saved as if was manna and they hadn't eaten for months.

WE WAITED UNTIL they finished eating before hearing their story, and it was a sad tale. The outward trip had gone well and they reached the Uua River before noon. They crossed over and travelled upstream to where Adune said there was an area of flat ground like we had described to him. It was easy getting out of the main river channel as the herds had broken down the banks in many places, although there were large boulder fields along the river bed. The river was about four hundred yards wide where

Wadis and scrub on the way to the Uua River.

they had arrived and it was difficult to find a clear route across because of the boulders.

On the far bank, going upstream, there were numerous feeder streams to cross before they reached the unbroken flat plain Adune had promised. When they did find it, the slope of the land proved to be very slight, less than a foot in eight hundred yards. This was unpromising for the kind of irrigated site we wanted to build. It would require a feeder channel several miles long just to bring the water to the surface. Adune said the ground was less flat downstream, so they turned around and headed south-east. He said there was a stretch where the river bottom was clear of boulders, suggesting that stronger flows, resulting from a steeper gradient, had scoured it clean. If the surrounding land conformed to the same profile it could suit our purposes much better. The drawback would be that some of the materials would need to be brought from further away, as we were proposing to use river boulders to construct our weirs. These would need to be carried in. Still, it was worth a look.

They found a possible site and there was enough evidence to suggest it would be worth coming back. Realising they had spent longer than they intended exploring the ground and would be making the last bit of their return trip in darkness, they wasted no time in crossing the river and heading back to camp, guided by Digeye and Adune.

There were a lot of little tributaries in this area and while trying to cross the third of these, the bank collapsed beneath the vehicle. As it slid sideways and backwards, the driver slammed the gear lever into four-wheel drive and piled on power. There was a jolt and a clang, the engine roared and the vehicle slid backwards to the bottom of a fifteen-foot gully.

It didn't take long to identify the problem as a broken half shaft in the back axle, and just as little time to realise that all the spares and tools had been unloaded when we camped and left behind when they set out for the Uua River. The Land Rover was going nowhere without some mechanical attention. There was no alternative but to walk back to camp, collect the tools and bring them back here to make repairs.

So they walked, heading south by the stars, following the two Afar men who didn't understand the inconvenience. They said they wouldn't normally travel at night, but there was a good moon rising, the sky was clear and there weren't too many thorn bushes in the area; why not walk? At least there would be food and water when they arrived.

"How long will it take to get to our camp?" Dr Abel had demanded.

The Afar looked at him curiously, not understanding his hurry. "Before the sun comes up, if you are not slow," they replied.

Hearing this, he decided to take the lead and set off at a furious

pace. The Afar ambled along behind. After a few hundred yards
he stopped and asked why they were not going faster. A discussion
between the Afar and Dagu went on for several minutes, involving
a fair bit of laughter. When they were done, Dagu turned to Dr
Abel and explained.

"They want to know if you can walk that fast for four days
and four nights without food or water."

"What's that got to do with it?"

"They say they can do this at the speed they walk and will
arrive before you. They will also avoid the snakes that wait under
the bushes at night to bite you and they will hear the hyenas
before they attack and be able to defend themselves. If you are a
clever man you will listen to them. This is their home and they
know it."

Dr Abel looked sour and deflated. He turned abruptly to
continue and walked straight into a thorn bush.

From then on either Digeye or Adune led the party. It soon
became apparent that their pace was not all that slow, but it was
constant, as was their chatter to one another. From the back,
Dagu joined in from time to time. Their course seemed erratic but
once again they were simply following the easiest route because
each time they came to another *wadi*, there was a convenient
crossing point in front of them which made it unnecessary to
search up or downstream for somewhere else where the bank had
collapsed.

As they neared our camp, it was even more obvious that the
guides knew where they were going as our shouts and waving
torches were directly in front of them.

2 ~ Drought and politics

THE DANAKIL DESERT, in north-eastern Ethiopia, is one of the most inhospitable places on the planet. It is the northern end of Africa's Great Rift Valley which stretches thousands of miles from Zimbabwe, up through Tanzania and Kenya to this corner of Ethiopia. Its northern end forms a broad depression that was cut off from the Red Sea millennia ago by a tectonic shift and volcanic activity. Much of it lies below sea level.

Even so, it has been inhabited for centuries by the Afar people who are secure in its arid inaccessibility and defend it against all comers with vigour and a certain barbaric flourish: until very recent times, they cut the genitals from the bodies of their enemies and wore them as ornaments.

To the north their principal opponents are the Eritreans, who would happily absorb into their own territory the salt mines which are the only economically productive part of the northern Danakil. For many years, Eritrea was part of the Ethiopian empire. Although it is largely desert and produces very little of value, the province was economically vital to Ethiopia since it contained the country's only two ports, Asmara and Assab, both of which lie on the Red Sea coast. Assab, the more southern of the two, is the principal point of entry for most of the country's oil supply. It is linked by rail and road to the rest of the country. The road runs slightly south of west, directly across the southern part of the Danakil to Bati, a small town perched in the foothills of the escarpment which forms the eastern rampart of the Abyssinian massif. It then meanders through tortuous mountains, zig-zagging up steep inclines with unprotected hairpin bends, to reach the interior.

I FIRST CAME TO the region in early 1973, when the drought was already well advanced and the Afar herds had lost over half their numbers. As well as all the animals, many people had died from thirst, starvation and disease. Those who survived were in a pitiable state, desperately in need of help and, unlike the mountain people, not even migrating to search for sustenance and support.

Being so fiercely independent, it never occurred to the Afar that by going elsewhere they might get help. In addition, moving into or through territory belonging to another tribe could be hazardous and none of them was in any condition to fight for free passage. So they stayed in their own lands, faced the situation with stoic fatalism and buried their dead in increasingly large clusters beside their encampments.

The need to be buried within their traditional tribal territory was another reason for not migrating in search of help. A sense of futility warned them that they were likely to die of the famine, so they preferred to do so at home. There was no religious requirement for this as the Afar people are nominally Muslim, although at that time few of them were devout, and held no religious ties to the land. It was something more fundamental, a residue, perhaps, of their tribal heritage from long before Islam arrived in their desert. Like many desert dwellers, these tribesmen had fought for their land and still held it with a territorial passion more familiar in other animal species. But, being in a marginal environment, where survival was always on a knife edge, they were reluctant to vacate any territory in case it was lost to them forever.

Ironically, even as they starved, there was food all around them if they had chosen to take it. Despite the drought, the Danakil desert still carried a healthy population of wildlife. Three kinds of gazelle, as well as ostrich and warthogs were common. The wildlife generally fared much better than the domestic herds. Because their population was less concentrated, their need for grazing imposed a less focussed burden on the sparse vegetation and they ranged more freely than the managed herds.

The Afar, however, had no tradition of hunting and ignored this meat supply, despite the fact that they do eat meat when their herds are plentiful. As a result, the wildlife is generally unafraid of humans. We found that it was often possible to walk within twenty or thirty yards of these animals before they turned and ambled away.

So the Afar stayed in their traditional lands, those who still had livestock helping those who had lost theirs, and they all suffered together. Hardly any of those who lived nearest to the road between Assab and Bati even bothered to visit the few small villages along the highway. Had they done so, their plight might have been noticed and reported by the police who manned outposts there or by the occasional truck or tanker driver who paused on his way to or from the port.

IN THE REST OF ETHIOPIA, which was itself struggling against the drought, nobody gave a thought to the Afar. The Galla people, who farm in the mountains to the west of the Danakil, are frightened of their fierce desert-dwelling neighbours and, since their superheated land held no general potential for farming, nobody wanted to go down there.

The few policemen at the isolated village posts along the Assab road generally assumed that they had been sent there as some sort of punishment. Indeed, in many cases this was true and they would be left alone until they had served their time in disgrace before, possibly, being brought back to the mountains and rehabilitated. They had no real duties to perform and no means of transport to get around the locality. So they simply stayed in their roadside posts and did nothing. Passing trucks dropped off rations for them about once a month and a superior officer was supposed to make an annual inspection visit, but this seldom happened.

In Ethiopia, exile to remote outposts, often after a spell in prison, was a common punishment for officials, politicians and other government servants who had fallen from grace or been caught up in any form of political activity that displeased the Emperor or his Rases. The Rases were princely warlords and provincial governors general, who controlled their fiefdoms with near-feudal power.

Since all the power was still concentrated at the top, it was difficult if not impossible to rectify wrongs. A man who had first-hand experience of this was Bimbashi Tefera Waldemariam, who became our District Governor in Bati.

As a young man, Tefera had been a high-flyer, holding a trusted position as commander of a troop in the Emperor's personal bodyguard. One day he insisted on disarming one of the Emperor's warlord cousins and his escort when they tried to attend an imperial audience without first surrendering their weapons. The Ras protested but Tefera insisted. The weapons were eventually surrendered and the visitors went in to their audience.

Political intrigue was rife in the Ethiopian court. The outraged Ras laid a charge against Tefera that resulted in him and all his troops being thrown into prison. Within a few days, before any protest he made could be heard, he was sent to work on a labour gang, building roads in the far south-west of the country, with a heavy ball and chain attached to his leg. Tefera knew that this was unjust, but his loyalty to the Emperor was unwavering, even though his protests went unheeded. He wrote to his master, but was carted off to prison even so. His letter, presumably, never reached the Emperor.

Two years later, the Emperor made a visit to the development project in the south-west. Tefera and his gang were resting under a tree nearby when the imperial helicopter landed, to be met by a fleet of cars. As the Emperor's cavalcade set off for the tour of inspection, somebody threw a grenade and shots were fired. The cars came to a confused halt with the imperial vehicle badly damaged. In that moment, Tefera leapt into action to protect his Emperor. He picked up his ball and chain, rushed towards the imperial car, smashed open the door and pulled the Emperor from the crumpled wreck. Still lugging the heavy ball and chain, he carried the Emperor, who was quite a small man, back toward the helicopter, dodging a fusillade of shots that were fired in his direction.

The pilot, having heard the explosion and the gunshots, was already restarting his engine as Tefera heaved the Emperor into the helicopter's cabin. A number of bullets smacked into the airframe. Pushing the dazed Emperor further inside, Tefera hastily climbed aboard himself, bringing his ball and chain with him, and slid the door closed as the pilot took off.

This action brought Tefera's case to the Emperor's notice in dramatic fashion, but the wheels of politics and justice grind in mysterious ways. For his bravery and loyalty, Tefera was immediately given an imperial pardon, but he could not return to his former position before other matters had been settled with the Ras who laid the original complaint. Instead he was promoted and posted to Bati as the new District Governor, with additional responsibility for the southern Danakil. But this was still in the future.

THE FIRST WORD THAT there might be something wrong in the Danakil only reached the local authorities in Dessie, the regional capital, about six months before Tefera earned his freedom. A policeman from one of the roadside posts hitched a ride up to Bati and reported sick. He was diagnosed with smallpox, which at the time was not unknown in the Horn of Africa. The governor of the day sent the man to Dessie for treatment and informed the regional authorities that a notifiable disease had broken out in the Danakil.

This gave an ideal excuse for people not to go there, but the Enderassie, the Provincial Governor in Dessie, did not want to be accused of doing nothing. He used his authority to summon a public health team and send them to travel the length of the road and find out if there was a general outbreak. Given the reputation of the Afar, the health workers were naturally reluctant to proceed without an armed escort so, after several weeks of dithering, one was grudgingly provided. It was made up of ten junior policemen with rifles.

In each village, the health workers used their escort to gather together any Afar who happened to be there. They then proceeded to administer smallpox vaccinations to everybody they had rounded up. The Afar I met later said they never even asked if anyone had the disease before they started to vaccinate.

The men, true to character, resisted and made it plain that they would fight, even in their starving condition; they were not going to be vaccinated. They gave way enough, however, to let their women and girls be treated. As soon as they had done everyone they could, the health team moved on, leaving a smart pink dressing on the arms of all the women and, such was their rush, a small pile of empty vaccine ampoules and used lancets lying on the ground where their work table had stood.

They hurried along the road, stopping for as short a time as possible in each of the tiny settlements, and were back in Bati three days later. The team members reported that they had encountered no smallpox among the Afar but had carried out a full vaccination campaign as a preventive measure. They didn't concern themselves with anything else, ignoring the all-too-evident hunger among the people because none of them had complained about it.

In each successive village they visited, the health workers encountered fewer and fewer people. Word had somehow gone ahead of them to warn of their coming and, after the way they had behaved at their first stop, Eliwoha, the Afar simply made themselves scarce until the intruders had moved on.

One of the health team drivers, Ato Jiorgiou Temennan, told a different story. Not being involved in the vaccination programme, he had wandered around and talked to those few people who spoke a few words of his native Amharic. From them he learned that the reason there were so few people anywhere along the road was because so many had died from starvation. He said the rest were hiding because they were suspicious of the government men with their armed escort. He had driven through the Danakil twice before and on both occasions had seen far more livestock and people about. Now the country looked particularly dry and empty. The truth, he claimed, was that the people and their livestock were starving and dying like flies because of the drought.

Needless to say, nobody in the regional capital took much notice of him; he was only a driver, after all. They accepted the health team's report and let the matter end there. It was not until a policeman sent through a report with one of the truck drivers that fifteen people had died of starvation near his post in Mille that anyone in authority even considered whether the desert might be affected by the drought that was causing so many problems in the rest of the country.

IN CHARACTERISTIC STYLE the authorities' response was ill-considered, inappropriate and grossly inadequate. To each of the three largest roadside villages, Eliwoha, Weranzo and Mille, they despatched a truck loaded with sacks of maize. With the truck went a gang of convict labourers to off-load them. The sacks were built into neat pyramids next to the police post in each village and covered with heavy canvas sheets. The policemen were told to keep an eye on the stack and prevent pilfering. Then the trucks returned to the mountains.

Five months later, when I arrived in the region, all this grain was still where it had been stacked, still neatly covered and baking in the merciless, searing sun. While the people got thinner, the rats and the pigeons got fatter. But the policemen did their duty and prevented anyone from pilfering.

The Afar never tried to steal any of the grain and probably wouldn't have done so even if it had not been 'guarded'. Apart from the fact that maize grain was useless to them as they had neither the means nor the knowledge to convert it to flour and cook with it, exposure to the heat of the sun for five months had destroyed any food value it might once have had. No distribution system had been set up and nobody had any authority to give the grain to those who needed it. The policemen were 'jobsworths' who wouldn't take any initiative except, perhaps, to pilfer some of the grain for themselves and to blame any shortage on the rats. It wouldn't have occurred to them to question why it was not being distributed. So it just stayed where it was.

WHILE ALL THIS was going on unseen down in the desert, the rest of the world was transfixed by daily television broadcasts from relief camps in the mountains. Images of skeletal children in their thousands, with long lines of patiently queuing people, all waiting in the desperate hope of a mouthful of food or some medical relief for their dying infants, filled the world's television screens and newspapers until the international community acted.

People in Britain rose to the occasion and donated millions of pounds for Ethiopian drought relief through the Disasters Emergency Committee (DEC), a group of major British charities and two government departments. Formed in 1963 in response to a severe cyclone in Sri Lanka, the DEC had been brought into action only once since then, in 1966. Then it was after an earthquake in Turkey in which 2,300 people died. Now, in response to dramatic television reports by Jonathan Dimbleby and others, they acted again, coordinating fundraising for a large group of British aid charities and collecting money through banks and post offices across the country.

There is nothing like a disaster, with all its potential for gruesome pictures and stories of terrible suffering, to attract the vultures of the world's press corps. The Ethiopian camps often had as many journalists as relief workers in them. The number of starving people rose by thousands every day until several million people were involved, many without the faintest hope of survival. The United Nations, as usual, stood on the sidelines and pontificated, coming late to the field and doing little to help until the western world's voluntary agencies had swung into action and were already hard at work on the ground.

The relief effort was massive and impressive. In a matter of weeks, food was pouring into the country, together with logistics specialists and health teams. Meanwhile, as word spread that relief was available in the camps, people began leaving their villages in the mountains and migrating in search of help, adding confusion to an already difficult situation and putting far more people at risk.

In areas where there were no roads and distribution by truck was impractical, mule trains began carrying sacks of food to isolated communities. One enterprising Swede, Count Carl Gustav von Rosen, who had been a mercenary pilot in Biafra during the conflict there a few years previously, arrived with a small fleet of light aircraft fitted with under-wing bomb racks. He had allegedly bought the aircraft with his own money and persuaded the Swedish government to bankroll his relief operation. He wrapped sacks of flour, milk powder and seed grain in rubber sheets so they would survive the impact and hung them on the bomb racks. Then he and his pilots 'bombed' isolated communities with supplies during low-level passes.

STILL NOBODY BOTHERED about the Afar, the 'people who wander'. Semi-nomadic herdsmen, the search for grazing keeps the tribes in the south of the region almost constantly on the move, their northern relatives less so. But gradually the reports from the Danakil by truckers about starving people gathering around the villages along the road began to be heard. Eventually some of these reports reached Addis Ababa, where somebody in the hierarchy asked questions. With no particular sense of urgency, the machinery slowly ground into action.

The authorities thought something could perhaps be done for the Afar that would ease the problem and keep them in their traditional lands. But the relief agencies were already overstretched and far too busy to extend themselves into what amounted to hostile territory. At the same time, the central government didn't want to be bothered with what it considered a minor provincial problem.

So the matter was passed to a minor agency, subservient to the Ministry of Agriculture, whose responsibility for the oversight of stock rearing throughout the country gave them nominal authority over the Danakil.

3 ~ A sort of a plan

SO IT WAS THAT the job which brought me to the Danakil was another of those inappropriate responses by people who were too lazy to find out what was actually needed but who knew that international opinion would condemn them if they did nothing. Someone in the central hierarchy in Addis Ababa decided that if the Afar had lost the stock upon which they depended for their livelihood, they needed to find a new form of subsistence or they would become a burden on the state which was ill-equipped and unwilling to support them. It would be a good idea if they grew food for themselves.

The fact that they inhabited one of the most hostile environments in the world meant nothing to the planners in Addis. They knew that on the Awash River, which flows through the most southerly part of the Danakil, there was an agricultural station and commercial cotton plantation at Dubti run by a British company, Mitchell Cotts. This was justification enough for uninformed administrators to decide that the rest of the region could grow food.

The mind-boggling stupidity of this attitude, and its

implications, are indicative of the time and place. It demonstrated their ignorance of the geography of the Danakil and lack of understanding of the massive foreign investment over many years that had been necessary to develop the Dubti enterprise.

The fact that, in all their history, only one of the Afar tribes had any agricultural experience or heritage, and that the use of tools was all but unknown to the vast majority of the Afar population south of the salt mines, didn't seem to register. The fact that the Afar lived in the hottest and driest desert on the planet, more than three hundred feet below sea level, where virtually nothing grew except spindly thorn scrub and occasional wisps of grass, didn't matter either. The fact that there was no usable surface water and no known subterranean aquifer suitable for exploitation, apart from in the Awash valley much further to the south, wasn't even considered.

What the authorities saw was that the changing weather patterns and resultant drought meant the days of viable animal husbandry for everyone living in the Danakil were over. Somehow they then made a mental leap to reason that a land that wouldn't support grazing could be made to grow crops. Agricultural self-sufficiency had to be the way forward for the Afar. This was the wisdom of the Livestock and Meat Board (LMB), the division of the Ministry of Agriculture responsible for oversight of the area they called the North East Rangelands.

THE LMB HAD NO proper maps of the area and little information on file about where and how the people lived. They certainly knew nothing about the different tribes, their structures and who the key people were. The only officials who ever went to the Danakil were veterinary officers who made occasional fleeting visits to guess at the condition of the livestock, or medical teams who had visited on the rare occasions that a notifiable disease had been reported. Even then, these people seldom ventured far from the road and never stayed more than a few days.

It turned out that the suggestion that growing crops might be feasible was developed after a couple of brief inspection flights had been made to verify stories about herds of cattle dying in the area. The plane's crew saw little of any herds but noted that the region was crossed by numerous dry river beds. This was corroborated by aerial photography, carried out in the late 1950s and early 1960s, which nobody had ever examined in detail. When somebody took the trouble to look, they found the photo mosaic showed the desert was indeed covered in dry water courses, originating from the foothills of the escarpment to the west. There must be seasonal rivers, the planners maintained, and these could be used to water the land for cultivation.

As hare-brained ideas went, this had to be one of the most brainless and nothing more was done to verify the assumption.

SO A PROJECT WAS conceived, help was sought from the British who would send a team out to choose suitable locations to build seasonal irrigation systems. The project was to be implemented in three phases: a brief reconnaissance phase; a surveying and planning phase; and finally, the construction phase.

The reconnaissance was to be carried out by a three-man team, two of whom would remain for the survey and design phase. One of these two would then stay to oversee the construction. The project was designed to run for about eighteen months and, once the Afar became involved and began to work, they would be paid for their labour with food. They would also be the sole beneficiaries of any crops that the project managed to grow. After that, government extension workers would take over guidance of the scheme and any continuation work.

The latter bit sounded to me most unlikely to happen, given the distinct lack of initiative or enthusiasm for working in the area up to this point. I suspected that the only reason anything was being done at all was because the key members of the project staff would be foreign-funded expatriates.

For many years the Ethiopian government, and in fact everyone else, had kept well clear of the Danakil and the Afar. The few outsiders who did go there went armed and prepared for trouble. As a result, trouble was generally what they got.

One who managed to return from the Danakil relatively unscathed was a young Englishman who was an intimate of the Abyssinian Imperial Court, where his father was the British Ambassador. In the early 1930s, he set out to travel the length of the Awash River to prove or disprove stories that the river disappeared in the desert and never reached the sea. His name was Wilfred Thesiger.

Although originally intending to go unaccompanied, Thesiger was required by the Abyssinian authorities to take an armed escort. The government was concerned lest anything should happen to him while he was among the lawless desert tribesmen. Not yet the self-assured independent explorer he became when he ventured into Arabia's Empty Quarter a few years later, Thesiger accepted the condition and took a company of fifteen well-armed soldiers. He ran his expedition along almost military lines, meeting every group of Afar that he encountered with an alert escort and a show of strength.

The Afar were wary of his soldiers and viewed Thesiger with

great suspicion. When they understood the purpose of his march, the tribes were determined to deny him access to the area where the true end of the Awash lies, almost as though it had mystical significance for them. After two and a half months of slow travel down the river, it took him a further two and a half months of patient negotiation, and more than a few bribes, before he persuaded the Afar sultan to let him explore the shores of the lake where he believed the river ended.

Eventually he managed to visit several of the lakes at the far end of the Awash – he told me about this when I sat next to him at a dinner in London in 1976 – but, by his own account in *The Danakil Diary*, which was not published until 1996, he was never wholly convinced that he had found the end of the Awash. Restricted in his investigations by the sultan and the local tribes, he had to accept the Afar's word that the river went nowhere else. The sultan insisted on driving him hastily out of his territory and onwards to Tajura, on the coast near Djibouti.

In the late 1930s, when the Italians colonised Abyssinia, they built the road which connects the Red Sea port of Assab to the nearest accessible part of the highlands at Bati. Because of attacks by the Afar, they lost more than four hundred construction men in three years, despite having regiments of trained troops as armed guards.

As recently as 1968, an Italian engineer and photographer named Giovanni Battista failed to return. He had been commissioned to travel the length of the road from Assab to Bati, to record its condition and that of the few settlements that had sprung up along its margins. Battista too travelled with fifteen armed guards and was reputed to be as adept at pointing a rifle as aiming his camera. When he reached their territory, the Adu

Aima'ara people took exception to him and his escort and sliced them up into little bits. The Adu Aima'ara's *makaban* was reputed to have worn the Italian's testicles as a necklace for several years after this event. When I met the same *makaban* in 1973, he was still proud of his part in this encounter. He had taken possession of the Italian's rifle which he showed to me, along with the six cowrie shells on his knife that signified the number of enemies he had despatched. Four of these, he said, had been members of Battista's escort.

After Battista, no outsider had ventured far beyond the fringes of the Afar territory and those Afar who came up to the markets on the edge of the escarpment were treated with wary suspicion.

Given this history, there was a distinct reluctance in official circles to allow anyone, particularly foreigners, to go down into the Danakil without a substantial armed escort. I had a problem with that: I was not in the habit of going round brandishing guns at people. It struck me that this could be seen as provocation and invite attack. It had, after all, happened before.

Our reconnaissance team, when we were all on the ground, discussed this matter at length while we spent three days poring over stereo aerial pictures to select likely sites worth investigation. We felt we should just take an interpreter and enough food and camping supplies for three weeks and go down and talk to the Afar and look at the land. Their help and involvement was going to be needed anyway and they were ultimately going to be the beneficiaries if the scheme worked, so why not make friends with the Afar at the beginning?

4 ~ The London connection

I ARRIVED IN LONDON after thirty-six hours of tedious travelling from central Africa via Liberia. Inbound from Bangui in the Central African Republic, I had been obliged to wait for twenty hours in Monrovia to catch my onward flight and had used the time by borrowing the customs officer's ancient typewriter and typing two reports, one on the project in central Africa I had been sent to set up and another for a different department. So when I arrived at the office in London's Victoria district, tired, dishevelled and in need of a bath, I was slightly disconcerted to be greeted by the doorman saying, "Good morning Mr Mathie. I thought you'd gone off to Ethiopia."

I dumped my suitcase behind the reception desk in the lobby, not intending to be there long, and headed upstairs to hand in my report and drop off the now wilting tropical blooms that I had brought all the way from the jungle for the girls in the typing pool. Elsa, the queen bee of the typists, welcomed me with a similar remark. "We thought you'd gone to Ethiopia," she said, "but thanks for the flowers." She had the courtesy to smile despite the bedraggled state of the blooms.

When someone else I hardly knew passed me in the corridor and asked, "Aren't you supposed to be in Ethiopia?" I smelled a rat. I marched into the divisional manager's office without bothering to knock and, with no ceremony or greeting, demanded, "What's all this crap about me going to Ethiopia?"

The manager looked slightly startled, his mouth gaping like a feeding carp. He glanced past me at an over-painted woman who occupied the armchair in his office. She spluttered at my abruptness and said sharply, "Young man, I don't think you should talk to your superior like that."

I rounded on her like a jackal before breakfast. "I don't give a toss what you think," I snapped back without thinking and barely looking at her. "I've no idea who you think you are, but this is none of your business," I turned my attention back to the man behind the desk who looked as if he was about to have a fit. "Well? What's going on, Gerald?"

"Behave yourself, Mathie," he spluttered. "This is our director, Mrs Anna Greening. She's in charge of this whole department, so mind your manners."

I looked more carefully at the woman. "Sorry, ma'am," I began, "I'm tired and wound up by all these people telling me I've been stitched up with something in Ethiopia. No offence meant. How d'you do?" I offered my hand. "I've also just hauled in from the middle of nowhere and need to hand over my report before I'm off on leave."

She heaved herself out of the armchair. "Call me Anna," she said as she shook my hand with a firm grip, then suggested that I come up to her office and have a cup of coffee. She'd soon get this Ethiopia business sorted out. "Anyway," she said, "I have a colleague upstairs who would very much like to hear a little about the mission you've just completed, before you go off anywhere, so perhaps you can spare him and me a few minutes."

I should have been suspicious when she mentioned the colleague, but was too tired to pick up the warning signal. "Fair enough," I mumbled, "put like that I suppose it would be rude to refuse. Sorry about snapping at you."

"Never mind that, let's go and get that coffee," she said, heading for the door like a galleon under full sail. "Thank you Gerry," she called over her shoulder as she led the way to the lift.

I dropped my project report on the manager's desk and followed meekly in her wake, feeling slightly foolish.

The directorial office was not as grand as I had expected. It was smart and well-appointed, yes, but functional too. I was to learn that this departmental director had a reputation for being a no-frills hard worker and this was quickly apparent. There was a meeting table set to one side with six chairs around it, one of which was occupied by a small grey man in a dull grey suit. There was nothing at all distinctive about him and this immediately made him distinctive to me. Apart from that, I knew who he was, although we had never been introduced, because I had seen him on a number of occasions in another government department that also made use of my services. I knew him by reputation too for, although one didn't talk about people like him, it was often what was not said that conveyed information and my friend and colleague Desmond had 'not said' quite a lot in the time I had known him.

WE STARTED WITH the mission I had just completed. After telling him the bones of it, I handed the grey man the second report I had typed while in transit in Monrovia. He perused this for a few minutes while I drank my coffee, then asked a series of questions.

Once it was clear that he had finished, I turned to the director and asked, "So what's all this about Ethiopia? I assume you have a project nobody else will touch and Gerald has landed me in it and said I'll take it, so what's the deal?"

She looked at the grey man who responded with a gargoyle-like grin. "I told you he'd see though it," he said. "He's not as thick as he looks; we wouldn't use him otherwise."

She heaved a big sigh, put down her coffee cup and told me. "Yes, you're right. It's something that's come up because of this drought and, rightly or wrongly, we are now committed to sending someone out there for a project which, in my opinion, is a waste of time. I'd like you to do it."

Well, that was honest, at least, and to the point.

She spent the next fifteen minutes filling me in on the background and then told me the deal. It didn't sound very savoury. Worse than that, it required someone to be on a plane that day as the rest of the mission had already been launched and I was the missing link.

I didn't admit it at the time, but I knew I was hooked and would do it. The calculating Mrs Greening knew it too but had the grace not to rub my nose in it. The grey man looked absolutely blank, but the very blankness of his face told me that he was the one who had set me up, had framed the whole deal and the way it was presented to me. He knew too much about me.

So we started haggling over terms of reference and time limits. Before I realised how much time had passed, a PA came in with a tray of sandwiches and more coffee. At about half past two, the director pressed a button on her desk console, asked her PA for some documents and a few moments later the girl appeared with a buff wallet file. As the director spread the contents on the conference table, I realised how sure they had been that I would accept the mission. The file contained a new passport in my name, already stamped with an Ethiopian entry visa for an unlimited stay. There was also an airline ticket and a few other things.

"We need to move on," said Anna. "Your plane leaves Heathrow in just over two hours. I'll take you out there myself and we'll continue the briefing on the way."

That was when I tried to throw a spanner into the works which I naively I thought might get me a few days' respite. I stated my price, saying that I required the whole fee to be paid up front and in my bank before I reached the departure gate.

The director never blinked. "I think we can do that, can't we?" she turned to the grey man who nodded his agreement. Damn, I thought, maybe I should have asked for more.

"Of course you will also be paid the usual per diem allowance, which we'll transfer into a local bank account as soon as you set one up and provide the account details," she finished off. This amounted to a further £13 per day. It doesn't sound much in today's money, but back then it was quite generous and I wondered if there'd be anywhere to spend it. Per diem payments were simply a standard rate living allowance for overseas staff. Best of all, you didn't need to provide any receipts.

"So, do we have a deal?" she asked.

"Almost," I said. "There's just one more thing: six weeks after I go out, I want you, personally, to come and visit."

"Me? Why?"

"You live here in this ivory tower, making decisions that affect people like me and those we work among. None of us believe you have the slightest clue what our work is about or what it's like living and doing what we do in the places we do it. We don't ask for much, but the few supplies or facilities we do request are all too frequently turned down." I had loaded the gun and now I paused to make sure she was following my reasoning before I pulled the trigger.

"Now, this is a deal breaker: you come out, without a lot of clap-trap, and spend a week with me in the desert, to see what it's actually like on the front line. If you don't come, I'll be on the return flight you should have arrived on and your project can whistle. His too." I waved my arm towards the grey man. He had been caught off guard enough to look mildly surprised. He knew I could be stroppy, but it had obviously never occurred to him I might hold anyone to ransom like this, especially the departmental director.

"Okay." Anna didn't waste time making up her mind and I wondered if she'd stick to the deal. She held out her hand to seal our bargain and I shook it. "Now, if you're ready, we need to go to the airport."

The grey man came with us. In the back of the Daimler as we travelled down the M4 to Heathrow, he briefed me on another mission that I was to carry out in parallel. I was to submit regular reports in a manner already well established and practised but the brief allowed me a lot of latitude in how I carried out the assignment. It was, of course, completely deniable. I knew the rules, there was nothing new in this, but they'd given me a legitimate reason for being on the ground and I saw no gaping holes in the rationale.

There was no discussion or negotiation this time; these were orders.

AT HEATHROW WE WERE met by another grey man, a younger one this time, with a briefcase. In a quiet corner, he handed an envelope to the first grey man who, in turn, handed it to the director. She handed it to me and told me to count it if I wanted to, indicating the airport branch of my own bank which stood a few yards away. I passed the unopened envelope through the teller's slot and gave her my account details.

As the clerk counted the money, I was aware of the second man hovering behind me. "Is there something you want?" I asked him.

"Depositing that amount of cash into a private account at the airport is likely to arouse suspicions. They'll probably need to run a check. I'm here to vouch for the payment and ease the process," he said and produced a rubber stamp from his briefcase.

As the teller finished counting and was stamping the receipt documents she looked up and asked if there was anything else I wanted. I told her the man next to me needed to speak to her about my deposit and he stepped up to the window, sliding something under the glass to her. She looked at it and slid it back with some other papers. He stamped and signed these, retaining two copies, one of which he passed to me. It was my receipt.

That was it. I had been paid. Now all I had to do was go to Ethiopia and build an irrigation system.

At that moment the final call for my flight came over the airport's loud speaker system. The director was still standing beside me but the two grey men were nowhere to be seen. As we shook hands Anna said, "Thank you, Ian. I'll see you in six weeks," then stepped back and waved me off.

I turned and went through the departure gate, not looking back, but sure she would remain there until I disappeared from view.

SITTING IN THE departure lounge, I had some more coffee and reviewed everything I had been told. I also considered how I had been stitched up and had a quiet chuckle to myself.

The drought had been in progress for some months and the international relief effort was already in full swing. The department was involved, both through the DEC and in its own right as an international aid agency. When the question of aid for the Danakil had finally surfaced, the Ethiopians had asked for help but there were political reasons why the government could not offer it directly. Instead they set up a complicated arrangement using third parties so that they could deny all responsibility and yet still have effective control. This I realised is how many governmental programmes work; it is one of the reasons why everything costs double what it needs to.

In this case they had farmed the project out through the Intermediate Technology Development Group and asked them to recruit an irrigation engineer for the first two phases of the work. Then, through channels of their own, the department had found a boffin from a top flight university with whom they had some obscure association and put him in for the first phase only. That left a place for one of their own field operatives, a man who was accustomed to working alone on development projects and delivering the goods regardless. His task would be to carry on and do the bulk of the work. There were eight people who met the criteria but none of the other seven was available or willing, so that third man was me.

As my flight was called, I remember thinking, 'What a complicated mess they've made of this. I'm glad I made the witch agree to come and visit. She won't like it.'

5 ~ Into the furnace

GOING THROUGH MY briefing notes again on the plane, I made a four-page list of factors that appeared to have been overlooked. None of the questions, it appeared, could be answered until we were on the ground in Ethiopia.

Our team of three had flown to Addis Ababa on separate flights and I was the last to arrive. After three days of uninformative briefings by officials at the Ministry of Agriculture and the LMB, and one tedious lunch at the British Embassy, we travelled by road up to Wollo, the province which includes the Danakil.

Our jumping off point for the Danakil was Bati, a small town on the escarpment above the edge of the desert where the weekly market is one of the biggest in East Africa, regularly attracting more than ten thousand people. We expected to continue the next day and descend into the desert, but the District Governor, Ato Giyorgis Gabre Yuhannou, had other ideas and insisted that nobody could go down to the desert without an armed escort. We would have to wait until he got authorisation for this from his superior in Dessie. He wouldn't permit us to go unprotected as there had recently been reports of fighting between the tribes. In addition, he had heard reports of Issa tribesmen making raids across the border from Somalia, which had caused fighting in one of the areas we proposed to visit.

We waited for eight days, doing nothing useful. The local LMB agent, Ato Habteab, had found us an Afar man called Dagu, who was to be our translator, so I spent time with him trying to start learning a little of the language. He was neither a willing nor a competent teacher and I soon found it more useful to wander around the market on my own and approach every Afar man I could find and try to talk to him. After four days, I found one who also spoke a little French. Unfortunately his knowledge was only rudimentary but at least it enabled me to learn a few of the greetings and one or two other words and phrases that might come in useful.

After a week of kicking my heels, I decided that inertia didn't suit. The others agreed, so we quietly fuelled and provisioned our Land Rover and late one night, much against the wishes of our driver, Elamu, who was terrified at the prospect of meeting the Afar, but with him at the wheel nonetheless, we set off down the tortuous road into the southern Danakil.

The first twenty miles of the road consisted of numerous tight bends, one leading into another with barely a few hundred yards between, on a steep gradient. It snakes its way down nearly seven thousand feet from the escarpment to the flat furnace below. There are almost no places to pull off the road and the outside of every bend is unprotected by any barrier, simply dropping off over a steep cliff. The Italian engineers who built it did a good job. It is well constructed with a good camber to keep vehicles on the road around the bends. In the darkness, it took us three and a half hours to drive down to the plain. We finally stopped at the first roadside village just after dawn.

SO BEGAN THE survey phase of a project in which I was supposed to construct, with Afar labour, at least one irrigation system that would catch the wet season flood as it poured down from the mountains. The idea was to divert the flood that was expected to flow down the innumerable dry *wadis* with weirs and channels into prepared basins where it would soak in and irrigate crops.

The theory, as far as it went, seemed plausible enough. There was evidence enough to demonstrate that the dry channels had, at some undefined time in the past, carried significant flows of water. In the mountains the rivers were known to flow strongly for seven or eight weeks every year and to trickle on for months after that. Until recently that is.

The mountains might have seen monsoon wet seasons in the recent past, but the desert itself had not seen rain for a long time. The climatologists' predictions were that rainfall delivered by the monsoon would be sparse for several more years yet before the weather cycles improved. They also predicted that in about ten years' time, the area would be experiencing another drought, affecting an even wider area. But nobody wanted to hear that; they were all too engrossed in the current emergency.

THE FIRST PROBLEM with the idea of capturing the runoff from the mountains and irrigating a patch of desert was that nobody had actually been down to the desert to see if the theory worked; to record where the water actually flowed and how it behaved when it did. Water can be unpredictable stuff and even moving slowly it exerts unimaginable forces on its surroundings.

The first task, therefore, was to find out how often any water came down the different dry river beds and try to assess how much it amounted to in each one. Then it would be necessary to locate possible places at which to build diversionary weirs and work out how much could be diverted and finally to design adequate bunded fields to receive it. On the expected volume of water would depend the area that might be irrigated, and on the profile and shape of the land would depend the size and layout of the field basins and the length of channels that would be needed to deliver water to the fields.

The whole task was made more difficult by the total lack of adequate maps. I had read unpublished reports about Thesiger's Danakil expeditions and had seen his maps, but the area where we were going was far to the north of where he had visited in 1934. Apart from a few aerial photographs and a couple of vague sketch maps, there was no topographical or cartographic data from which to select possible areas for inspection. There was also no satellite navigation system by which to find our way around the desert – that hadn't yet been invented. The only way to find places was to get out on the ground and take a look at the land, having first identified possible locations from a set of twelve-year-old aerial photographs which would probably bear little relation to the ground as it now was. I was glad that I had thought to bring a sextant and a set of navigational tables; this at least gave some sense of order to our navigation and enabled us to fix the locations of any potential sites we did find.

AT THE POINT WHERE the winding mountain road flattened out onto the desert floor, a spring with good fresh water trickled from the rocks a few yards from the road. Everyone going down this road stopped here to fill their water tanks before crossing the desert as there would be no more surface water until Assab, on the Red Sea coast. The water was surprisingly cool and quite potable. Desert water in most other places varied from being slightly brackish to tasting like Epsom Salts. This was sweet water.

It was perhaps more surprising that no community had grown up around this spring, but the place was deserted. There was simply a small flat area beside the road, big enough for three cars and a lorry to stop, with a cliff behind it and the water dribbling out of a crack in the rock. The only development that had been done on the source was a small stub of pipe jammed into the rock so that the water came out in a small fountain, rather than just running down the face of the rock. It still drained away into cracks between jumbled rocks beside the bottom of the cliff and vanished somewhere under the road.

We had descended almost to sea level at this point. It was a lot hotter down here than it had been up on the escarpment, even in the early hours before sunrise. We all drank freely in the pre-dawn gloom and filled every container we carried before driving on east, towards the lightening horizon.

Dawn came suddenly, just before six o'clock. For a few moments there was a thin grey line on the distant horizon. This changed almost imperceptibly to a narrow orange glimmer and expanded during the next three or four minutes to become a wide orange glow that extended upwards as the sun approached the horizon. Since we were heading east, all this was ahead of us. For a few moments the road became indistinct as the headlights no longer had the power to illuminate it. Then the sun burst from its concealment as if an orange flood light had been turned on and was climbing a gantry to soar magnificently clear of the earth.

Within seconds the brightness increased, the warm orange changed to a glaring gold, too bright to look at and the first of the sun's warmth reached us like a soft breeze.

The glare right in his eyes was too intense for our driver, who stopped the Land Rover and said we would have to wait for at least fifteen minutes as he couldn't see where he was going. He pulled off onto a flat silt pan beside the road and we all climbed out to stretch our legs.

This was indeed an arid place, with a few small sun-blackened rocks scattered across the ground and occasional spindly thorn bushes about eight feet high. The soil was soft to the touch and pale grey in colour for as far as we could see. There was no sign of grass or even the candelabra *Euphorbias* that had been so plentiful on the rocky slopes we had passed during our descent from the mountains. Even in the darkness we had been aware of their gaunt shapes scattered across the hillsides like sombre black ghosts, their arms upraised in supplication to a celestial entity in the star spangled blackness above.

Within minutes of the sun clearing the horizon, the desert began to reflect its radiated heat and the slight shimmer of heat haze began to distort the view and shorten our perspective. I looked around, half expecting people to appear out of the landscape. Anywhere else in Africa, a Land Rover stopping by the roadside acted as a magnet for people who came, either holding out their hands to ask for something, or just to stand and look and watch. But this place was deserted. Nobody came. Their absence felt singularly eerie and odd.

The road was not as well-maintained here as it had been on the mountain section and its surface was lumpy and uneven. Because of this, it took a further hour to reach the first of the permanent

Eliwoha police post and the pyramid of grain.

villages, Eliwoha. To call the place a village was perhaps a misnomer as it consisted of no more than fifteen crude huts made from sticks and pieces of beaten metal scrounged from old oil drums, panels off dead vehicles and anything else that might offer a little protection from the sun and the searing wind. The only permanent building was the police post and even this was run down and dilapidated. Apart from the flag pole in front, it was, at first sight, hard to distinguish from the other huts in the village.

Behind the police post was a small pyramid, covered with a new looking green tarpaulin. This was the load of grain that had been dropped off five months previously, supposedly to feed the starving people. Its base was surrounded by a meagre fence of thorny branches, torn from the nearby bushes.

I wandered over to look at it and the policeman, attentive to his duty, immediately came to see what I was doing. I asked him how long it had been there and what instruction he had received about it. He explained how it had been delivered and said he had been told to look after it and not let anyone touch it. I asked how much had been distributed.

"None," he said.

"Why not?"

He told me that he was ordered to look after it and stop people stealing it, not to distribute it. So there it sat, baking in the sun.

Some way to the north of the village, about four hundred yards from the road, was a cluster of small brown domes, about five feet high and eight or nine feet in diameter. These were Afar huts, called *a'ari* by their inhabitants. There was nobody to be seen near the huts but one or two Afar men were standing about idly near the road. They were distinctive with their white clothes, dressed hair and *gillés*. They stood about striking poses, watching us from a distance. The interpreter told us these people were men of the Meklet clan, from the Abu Sama'ara tribe.

On this first occasion, we didn't stay long at Eliwoha but pressed on further into the desert. We intended to turn off the road about fifty miles further on and travel north toward an area where we hoped to find suitable sites for our irrigation project near the Uua River. There was no actual river there, of course, but local hearsay told us that this was one of the channels most likely to carry water from the escarpment even in the driest years. From this uncertain knowledge and the apparent expanse of the flat land nearby which we had been able to identify from the aerial photos, together with the reports of a survey pilot four years previously that he had seen large herds of cattle in the area, it seemed like a reasonable place to start. Large herds suggested that there had been good grazing and good grazing for cattle meant there must have been grass. That sort of grass doesn't grow without water, or so our reasoning went.

That is how hit-and-miss this whole escapade was at the beginning. Based on such scant information, we were willing to launch ourselves into the unknown in 'hostile' territory. I can imagine how Fawcett must have felt as he set out in search of Eldorado, only we had no rich prize at the end of our quest.

The road improved sufficiently after we left Eliwoha for us to maintain a respectable forty miles per hour. The land on either side rose and fell no more than a hundred feet in a few isolated places and was otherwise flat and empty to the shimmering horizon. The horizon was not, in fact, that far away, being obscured by intense heat haze within an hour of sunrise. Since we had spent the best part of an hour at Eliwoha, the road dissolved into a wobbling miasma less than half a mile ahead of our windscreen. We travelled with all the windows and scuttles on the Land Rover open, hoping that the small currents of air generated by our forward progress would offer some cooling, but the temperature inside rose inexorably and it was not long before we were sucking on our water bottles and discussing whether we would need to ration our supply.

At mile forty-eight after leaving Eliwoha, we got a puncture in the front left-hand wheel. The vehicle slewed violently off the road, bumping over the stones that formed a kerb and grinding to a halt, its nose pointing downwards into a gully that was presumably built as a storm drain.

There was a spare wheel on the bonnet and two more under our camping gear on the roof rack. The jack, when we finally unearthed it under the baggage in the back, had a tooth missing from its cog, which made cranking it up a slow and hazardous business. After turning the handle seven-eighths of the way around, we had to jam rocks under the raised axle to stop it slipping back and then ease the crank past the broken tooth before winding it hard again to raise the vehicle a little more. Lowering it back onto its wheel once the punctured tyre had been changed was just as hazardous and slow.

It took more than an hour to change the wheel, with all of us taking turns at the work. By the time we finished, the sun was high overhead and there was almost no shade except directly beneath the Land Rover. We decided to pull onto the flat and rest for a couple of hours, spreading a fly sheet over the vehicle with a supporting pole at each corner. We pulled it out to one side to give us enough shade to put out camp chairs.

In the heat none of us really wanted to eat, so we just sat and dozed. The slight breeze that we hadn't noticed before dried the sweat from our limbs and slowly desiccated us. When the sun started to creep around the end of the vehicle at about three

Broken ground south of Eliwoha, dotted with thorn scrub.

o'clock, we took down the awning, strapped it and the poles back on the roof and moved on.

It was as we started packing up our gear that we noticed the first flies. They had been unusually absent up to this point but now a few arrived and started buzzing round us. The few were soon followed by the many and by the time we were driving again we were all batting at the cloud of them that invaded the boiling Land Rover cabin and swarmed around us. It was a hopeless task, like trying to slay the Hydra, for as soon as we killed one fly a dozen more replaced it. We drove on in this misery for about twenty minutes and then, as suddenly as they had appeared, the flies vanished. We had no idea why and wondered if flies can be territorial.

Driving over the open land was much slower than on the road. We had to cross the frequent dry gullies which occasionally were deep enough to have vertical banks ten or twelve feet high. Then it was necessary to drive along the bank until a suitable crossing point was found where it had collapsed. Often enough this didn't correspond with a similar incline on the other side and so we had to drive up or down the channel to find an exit. This made forward progress across the landscape very slow.

By dusk we had covered less than twenty miles and we had seen nobody. We had passed occasional small groups of Soemering's gazelle and a couple of ostriches but had seen no livestock and no domed huts to indicate the presence of people. As the sun lowered itself towards the horizon, we stopped and made camp near a thicket of spindly camel thorn bushes.

Once the sun set, the transition from bright daylight to full darkness took less than ten minutes. Soon the sky overhead was blazing with stars, bright enough for us to see much of what we were doing without needing lamps. Despite the many times I had seen this before, the spectacle never ceased to enthral and delight me. The other two members of our team were new to Africa so this was a novel experience and its wonder was not lost on them.

FOR CONVENIENCE on this reconnaissance trip, we were feeding out of tins, so supper did not take long to prepare. By the time the moon rose, less than two hours after we had stopped, we had all eaten and were discussing how to go about the preliminary survey we hoped to make the next day. By nine o'clock we were ready to sleep but the temperature was still over a hundred degrees Fahrenheit and we all felt like limp rags. We sat in our camp chairs hoping to catch any night breeze there might be and dozed, eventually lying down on camp beds beneath the two fly sheets we had put up when we stopped.

This was our first night in the Danakil, the beginning of a new project, a whole new adventure, and the point at which this account started.

6 ~ A solution, desert style

WITH THE OTHERS back in camp after their midnight walk, our discussion turned to what to do about the broken Land Rover. We had already discovered that everything that happened here was to become the subject of intense and protracted discussion and negotiation, so it was no surprise that this simple matter resulted in so much argument, even among us three Europeans. In the end we agreed that after everyone had eaten and slept, half of us would walk back to where the vehicle stood, taking tools and spare parts with us and do something about recovering it.

Opinions on how this should be done differed as Dr Abel insisted that it needed a full repair before it could be driven at all. Elamu and I had other ideas and I found myself wondering again where London had found this odd man and why he was even here.

As everyone was settling down to sleep after eating, I took Dagu and Digeye aside and had a short discussion. Then we went back to the group and sat down to rest. As soon as the others were asleep, I woke the two men and Elamu. Quietly we gathered a selection of tools from the box we had off-loaded and put them in a canvas bag. Then I picked up the small hand winch and a long corkscrew anchor together with three full water bottles. The four of us set off without waking the others.

It was faster walking in daylight and it took us only three hours to reach the Land Rover. We found it sitting at a precarious angle, looking like it was ready to topple onto its side. We had to dig soil away from one side and level it before anything else could be done. Digging was extremely hard work in the heat. It was made only slightly easier by the fact that the soil was light and not too compacted. Nevertheless, we could dig for only about ten minutes before needing water and a rest. This dusty task gave me a good idea of what we were to face once the construction phase of our project started.

By the time the Land Rover was safe from toppling, we were all tired, but that was the more difficult part of the job done. The vehicle's position on the slope meant that access to the underneath was now quite easy and so the next task, to unbolt the prop shaft that connected the gearbox to the rear axle, could be done without having to jack it up to reach underneath. It only required the removal of eight bolts to dismount the drive shaft and it should have been a quick job, but we soon realised that although this vehicle had a full maintenance record, nothing had been done to it for a long time. It certainly hadn't seen a grease gun recently. The bolts were badly corroded, caked in an old accumulation of hard dirt. It took more than an hour to undo all eight of them and to remove the prop shaft.

Extracting the two stub axles from the rear wheels took another two hours, by which time the sun had passed its zenith and was losing its intensity. It would soon be going down. We needed to get the Land Rover out of the gully and up onto the flat land before the light went. With the rear axle disconnected and the gears set in low ratio four-wheel drive, the power from the engine all went to the front wheels. With a little help from the hand winch, it would be relatively straightforward to drive up onto the stream bank, or so we hoped.

We twisted the corkscrew anchor into the flat ground well ahead of the vehicle and hooked up the winch cable. The winch itself was bolted onto a bracket on the front bumper of the Land Rover. As Elamu put it in gear and lifted his foot from the clutch, I cranked the winch handle. Slowly the grumbling vehicle climbed out of the wadi and ten minutes later it stood on level ground. By the time we had collected all our tools and equipment, the sun was below the horizon and darkness was upon us again.

Using the Land Rover as a front-wheel drive vehicle and taking it slowly, we made good progress. Digeye was an excellent navigator and understood that we needed the easiest possible crossings at each gully we came to. Two hours later, after crossing a total of thirty-nine dry stream beds, we drove back into our camp to the intense relief of those waiting for us. They had been irritated to wake and find us gone, but their relief at our return soon defused most of the tension. The only person to comment was Dr Abel. I thought this was a bit rich since he had done nothing but complain since we set out from Addis.

That evening around the camp fire we reviewed our situation. The unfortunate incident had taken more than a day out of our planned trip and we were committed to being back in Bati quite soon. In addition, Dr Abel was supposed to be with us for only two weeks and it would take at least thirty-six hours to get him back to Addis Ababa in time to catch his flight home. Time was running out.

From the provisional list we had made at the beginning, we

selected two more sites in this part of the desert that might be worth investigating. These lay on a route that would take us back to the main road in less than two days. One of them was still in the Dodha tribe's territory and, with only a little persuasion, Digeye and his companions agreed to act as our guides. It would be an uncomfortable crush in the vehicle, and they were still very aromatic, but Bruce and I felt that having them with us was worth the discomfort. The opportunity to earn some money and be fed while they were with us was a persuasive factor and we learned a little more about negotiating with the Afar.

The first location proved to be a waste of time and we decided to head due south and pick up the main Assab-Bati road in order to go and look at the other place. Soon after we set off, however, Bruce noticed a number of mature acacia trees some way off to our left which suggested that there might be either a water hole or a source of underground water nearby. While these trees are known to have deep tap roots, they only grow to this size when water is plentiful. They are quite slow growing and these were big trees, at least sixty feet high, so we diverted to have a look.

It took only moments to realise that this place offered much better potential than anything we had see so far, so I got out the sextant and fixed our position. We agreed to make this one of the first visits for the next phase of the mission. This done, we headed south again and found that the main road was a lot nearer than we expected.

The village of Weranzo turned out to be only fifteen kilometres away. Finding this was akin to finding an oasis with palm trees and a cool lake in the middle of the Sahara. Besides the police post and a few ramshackle huts, there was a bar with a paraffin-operated refrigerator and cool drinks. Better still, the man who

Fred's Bar
Naravzo
24·8·74

owned it had recently stocked his refrigerator with cans of beer.

The owner seemed a genial sort. "What is his name?" we asked our Afar companions. Their response was unpronounceable.

"Fred," suggested Bruce.

"Fred it is," I agreed, and Fred he became thereafter.

Our presence led to a number of curious Afar appearing out of nowhere. They clustered around to look at us and to ask our companions who we were, what we were doing there and what they were doing in our company. We bought coffee and food for the five men who had been our guides and passed packets of Ethiopian-made Nyala cigarettes around those watching, while Digeye and his friends told all they knew about us and then asked if there was anyone in the village who came from the neighbouring Abu Sama'ara tribal area.

By chance there was one man so we immediately began negotiating with him to be our guide for the next stage of the survey. He was wary and, because the man who had told him what we were doing had been from the Dodha tribe, he distrusted what he had been told. He insisted on being told what we were doing and why by us, through our own translator who came from a different tribe which was situated further away and therefore had no interest.

This level of inter-tribal distrust was another factor that the briefings had not warned us about. It too became a feature of our dealings with the Afar. Before long, I was accustomed to explaining the same thing ten or fifteen times just to find the right person with whom to begin any meaningful discussion. Any idea I might have had of activities involving more than one tribe were clearly not viable.

After an hour and a half of talking, the man, whose name was Hamire, agreed to be our *aban* and take us to meet his *makaban*. It was the first time I had heard these terms and I asked Dagu what they meant. He explained that an *aban* was a guide who ensured safe conduct. The *makaban,* among these southern tribes, was the ultimate leader of any group. It was both a clan and tribal position. There was also someone known as the *balabat*, who was supposed to have some influence but, as he was a paid government appointee, he held little or no respect among the people and was unable to exercise much authority. This did not mean that the *balabat* was of no significance and could be ignored. I discovered during subsequent discussions that the Afar would hide behind the *balabat*, saying he needed to be consulted and give his approval, whenever they were unwilling to make a decision or a commitment. Since on these occasions the *balabat* was invariably absent, the delay until he could be found and consulted gave them additional thinking time and manoeuvring room and frequently resulted in the whole discussion having to be run again. It was an interesting negotiating tactic and I wondered how a British factory would function if the trades unions adopted it.

We asked if the man he was going to take us to meet was a tribal or a clan *makaban*. Hamire said he didn't know and he didn't seem disposed to explain. This obtuseness illustrated another Afar characteristic.

After giving Hamire a cup of coffee to seal the deal, we paid off our first group of Afar guides. I told Digeye that we would meet him again at Weranzo when Bruce and I returned in a week or so, and that we would employ him as our *aban* again. He said that if he wasn't there, I should ask the bar keeper and word would be sent to him. He and Fred obviously knew one another well.

Dagu chose this moment to take a break from the job. He admitted that he didn't want to go with us to meet this new *makaban* because he was likely also to meet another man with whom he had an ongoing disagreement and he did not want to get into a fight.

It now looked as if our trip to meet the Abu Sama'ara *makaban* was destined to be a waste of time but Hamire told us the man spoke good Amharic and would be able to talk to our driver. We asked Elamu if he was willing to try and interpret and he agreed.

As it happened, our trip to talk to the Abu Sama'ara did indeed turn out to be a complete waste of time, but for a different reason. After a long discussion, the *makaban* to whom Hamire introduced us told us that the location we wanted to survey was not in his clan's territory and therefore he couldn't give us permission. He gave the name of another man we should talk to but said that this chap had recently gone away to find grazing and wouldn't return for at least three weeks.

With time running out, we decided to abandon any idea of surveying on the Jeldi Plain, and two other locations further south towards the Awash River valley that were also in Abu Sama'ara territory, and to return to Bati.

The road back east took us once more through Eliwoha and we stopped there to make enquiries at the police post. The policemen didn't know anything that might be useful to us but Dagu, who had resumed being our translator once he discovered the man he was afraid of was away, found two men who knew the *makaban* we had been told to speak to. They assured us that the Jeldi Plain was part of their own clan territory and the man had authority over it. The only problem was that this *makaban* had gone to Bati, hitching a ride on a petrol tanker that stopped in Eliwoha the day before. One of the men offered to come with us and make the introduction, saying we could bring him and the makaban back here if we still wanted to talk to them. I wondered momentarily why we couldn't simply talk to the *makaban* in Bati, but then realised that the rest of the clan would need to be consulted. Nothing was ever decided by a single person among these Afar.

Dr Abel decided this sounded to like nothing more than a roundabout way of the man getting a lift to the market, four or five days walk away, and he would have nothing to do with it. Apart from that, four hours incarcerated in the vehicle with the aroma of sheep's butter was more than he was prepared to tolerate. Climbing onto his high horse, he wouldn't budge. He was already cross with me for leaving him and Bruce in camp with four tribesmen and going off on my own to rescue the Land Rover without telling them.

We argued for twenty minutes and finally I offered to leave him and Bruce in Eliwoha while I took the man to Bati and fetched his *makaban*. The prospect of being left in this scruffy little village was worse than the prospect of the ride and he reluctantly climbed into the vehicle, sitting as far from our guest as possible, with his head out of the window. I don't think he ever forgave me and by the time we got to Bati, his face was badly scorched by the sun and the hot wind of our passage.

True to his word, the man did introduce us to his *makaban*, an older man of about fifty, who listened to what I explained and finally said he would be willing to discuss the matter with us among his people. He would be back in Eliwoha in nine days and we could come and see him and the other elders then to talk about it. This seemed remarkably decisive after some of the evasive responses we had received before, but Dagu assured me the man meant what he said. We shook hands and parted, driving round to the small hotel where we had spent the week before going down to the desert to see if we could get rooms and the use of a shower.

News travels fast in frontier towns. We had been at the hotel less than an hour before a summons arrived from the District Governor. He was clearly none too pleased at our ignoring his edict not to go into the Danakil without an armed escort and was demanding an explanation.

"We'll be more comfortable and presentable if we have a shower and a meal before going to see the governor," I suggested. It was already late afternoon and we were covered in Danakil dust. That was not the best way to face what was inevitably going to be an awkward situation, so we agreed to clean up, eat and go later. The governor had previously told us that his office was always open until late evening as it was more comfortable to work in the cooler hours, so the delay should cause no problem.

By the time we got to his office, the sun was sliding behind the mountain ridge to the west and the building was locked up. I asked the guard on the gate what time the governor had gone home and was told that he had left immediately after sending us a message to come and see him, earlier in the afternoon. He had said the inconvenience would teach us something. I thought about this for a moment and then wrote a message on the back of the governor's summons telling him we had called and returned to the hotel. We would be there until seven the following morning and were then heading up to Dessie and Addis Ababa. If he wanted to see us, he was welcome to visit us at the hotel. I put it in the envelope and asked the guard to give it to the governor when he returned.

We left at seven the next morning without seeing any sign of the governor. Saying goodbye to Dagu, we paid his wages and gave him five kilos of rice as a bonus, telling him Bruce and I would return in ten days for the next stage of the mission. He said he would be here and looked happy as he waved us off.

THE TRIP BACK to Addis Ababa was tedious, taking almost thirty hours. This was partly due to our detour to Dessie, to visit the LMB office there and find out what construction supplies might be available locally. It was also because we got caught behind an overloaded wagon that crawled along the winding mountain road up to Kombolcha. With the Land Rover stuck in front-wheel drive and consequently limited on speed, there had been no way of passing it for almost twenty miles. When we eventually came to a small village only a few miles short of the town, the wagon stopped and we were able to get past and go a little faster. Even so it didn't make much difference as we still had to get up the twisted road to Dessie and back down again before continuing south.

The next slow section was where, having dipped down after ascending the first step of the foothills, the road climbs nine thousand feet up the edge of the great escarpment from Debre Ziet to Debre Berhan. It snakes back and forth across a six-mile section of the escarpment, around tight hairpin bends, finally to disappear after the last climb into a tunnel that goes straight through the mountain and emerges on the plateau a few miles north of Debre Berhan.

It is a slow and nerve-wracking climb at the best of times, starting among sweet-scented glades of fig and eucalyptus trees but all too soon emerging into the glare of the sunlight a third of the way up the incline. The slopes above are largely bare, with signs of frequent rock falls leaving long chutes of scree that reach down to the road like threatening warty tongues. It is not unknown for large lumps of rock to come crashing down onto the road, knocking vehicles over the edge. A litter of ancient wrecks further down bears mute testimony to this and, since the edges of the road are unprotected by crash barriers, vehicles could equally be pushed over the edge while trying to avoid oncoming traffic.

We stopped in Debre Berhan for fuel, a walk round and a meal. The only food available was the traditional Ethiopian fare of *injera* and *wat*. This looks remarkably unappetising but it is actually quite tasty. *Injera* is a traditional form of bread made from *teff*, a small grass whose seeds grind down to pale grey flour. When mixed with finely chopped onions and water and allowed to ferment for a few hours, it becomes a thick soupy paste. Once it is ready, this mixture is poured in a spiral motion onto a hot metal plate, about eighteen inches in diameter, which is placed over a small pile of burning charcoal. The centre of the plate gets very hot, its outer edges less so. Pouring starts at the outside edge and by the time the spiral reaches the middle, the outside is cooked, forming a thin sheet of rubbery bread that looks for all the world like a vast grey crumpet, complete with little holes. It has the consistency of that kind of foam rubber that was used to fill cushions and pillows in the 1960s and has a sour taste which is dispelled by dunking it in hot spicy stews and sauces.

The *wat* component of the dish is a simple stewed sauce made with meat, fish or vegetables. It is invariably strongly spiced, usually with chilli. You place a dollop of *wat* in the centre of the *injera* and fold it inward over the top. Placed in a lidded basket about ten or twelve inches across, it makes a conveniently portable package for a meal that you can eat hot or cold.

Dr Abel was getting increasingly uncomfortable with Ethiopia. Now he was unhappy about Elamu sharing food with us, although he had been doing so throughout our time together. He considered Elamu to be just a driver, rather than a member of the team and said he ought to eat separately, as befitted his station. Added to this, he didn't like the food or anything else we encountered along the way, so by the time we finally got back to the capital we were all fed up with his continuous carping. He was still complaining when we reached the hotel later that evening and went straight up to his room.

Bruce and I helped Elamu unload and put our kit into the hotel store. We then sent him home for the night with the vehicle, asking him to collect us at nine the following morning.

We had a couple of minor functionaries from the British embassy as company for breakfast the next day. It transpired that Dr Abel had been on the phone to them the night before, insisting they should join us so that he could hold court. It was clearly important for him to have the opportunity to polish his ego and tell them what a hellish time he had had in the Danakil before getting on the plane to return to London. I listened in amazement as he made no mention at all of the useful work we had done or of anything we had learned about the Afar and their situation. He just droned on about the heat, his discomfort and the thorns.

While the diplomatic team admitted none of them had yet been down to the Danakil, I marvelled that he could think they were quite so unaware of what the country was like. The fact that he conveyed no useful information seemed to bypass the two diplomats who sympathised sycophantically and ate their free breakfasts as if they too were victims of the famine.

Elamu arrived at nine with a different vehicle. He had taken the first one back to the ministerial motor pool to get the back axle changed. When I asked him if he was in any trouble over the breakage he said no; since he had not been driving when it happened, he was not deemed to be responsible. Up to this point I had not been aware that someone else had been driving and when I asked who it was he said, "Your boss man."

"Boss man? We don't have a boss man."

"That doctor thinks he is the boss. He said he could drive the Land Rover better than me and insisted I let him do it. He thinks he is superior to everyone, but really he is very ignorant. I have not enjoyed working with him." Elamu looked slightly embarrassed as he said this and quickly followed it with, "Please, I don't want to make trouble, but it has been difficult."

Such a disclosure from anyone who was employed in a job like his was truly exceptional here but it gave me a good insight into the relationship Bruce and I had formed with him. I assured him there wouldn't be any trouble. The next phase of the project would only involve me and Bruce and we would pick up Dagu in Bati. We were going to be down in the desert for less than a month. Elamu had done a good job with us so far and we would be pleased to have him along for the next phase if he was willing to come. He looked relieved and welcomed the opportunity to be part of our team. He cheered up even more when Dr Abel announced that he wouldn't be coming with us to the LMB office that morning; the embassy staff would drive him out to the airport.

We left the stuffy doctor at the hotel and went to work, with Elamu humming quietly to himself as he drove us through the crowded streets.

7 ~ Survey

AFTER THREE DAYS OF pointless meetings with the LMB in Addis Ababa and the development attaché from the British Embassy, who contributed little of value, Bruce and I returned to Bati, taking Elamu with us again as our driver and general handyman. We spent the first half of the morning stocking up on provisions and settling a few administrative arrangements, then headed north before anyone else could demand our time. We were supposed to spend just under four weeks on the surveying phase but the time wasted in the capital had already eroded that. Now, with three locations identified as being worth further investigation, we were keen to get back and start work.

We planned to start with a site in the far south, by the Chelaka River, one of the almost permanent tributaries of the Awash which we had heard about but not yet seen. After inspecting that, we would survey the site we had found just north of Weranzo and then, if time and the Afar permitted, one on the Jeldi Plain.

We arrived in Bati and checked into the hotel half expecting to receive a demand for our presence from the District Governor, but no messages awaited us. Neither was there any sign of Dagu. We rested the first night and spent the following day sorting out aerial photos of the sites we proposed to survey, using them and tracing paper to make a map and setting out a work plan. Bruce and I spent a few hours working with the dumpy level and measuring staff in a nearby orchard to make sure that we understood one another's signals. When we were satisfied that we both agreed the procedures, we went through our kit and, with Elamu's help, carefully packed the Land Rover so that there would be the minimum of unpacking and unloading each time we stopped. We bought two extra ten-gallon water carriers in the market and finally visited the District Governor's office to let him know we intended going down into the Danakil again.

The governor was not there. After a while the guard took pity on us and told us that he was not even in Bati; he had been called to Dessie and word had later come back saying that he had then gone up to Addis Ababa.

When would he be back?

Nobody knew.

Back at the hotel, there was a message from Dagu saying he had gone back to his home in the north. Now we had no translator. I asked the local LMB official, Ato Hapteab, if he knew of another, but he didn't. There was nothing for it, so I went to the market and walked around looking for any Afar man I could find who might speak a bit of French.

I didn't find one, but I did find Mohammed Asif, an Afar from the northern region who had spent some time at a rare Christian mission school and spoke quite good English. Better still, he needed a job. I took him back to the hotel and introduced him to Bruce and Ato Hapteab. It only took a few minutes to arrange his employment and we were ready for the desert. All we needed now was the governor's clearance, but he still wasn't back and nobody had the faintest idea when he would come.

Over supper that evening, Bruce, Mohammed, Elamu and I discussed what we should do. We were all agreed, governor or no governor, we had a job to do. After supper I paid our hotel bill, told the proprietor that since the governor was away we had decided to go up to Dessie early the following morning and if anyone wanted us, that's where they should look.

At three the following morning, we quietly climbed into the Land Rover and let the brake off. It rolled half a mile down the hill and round two bends before Elamu started the engine, confident nobody would hear it start. Before dawn we stopped at the spring beside the road and topped up all our fresh water containers and long before the sun was an hour into the sky we had passed through Eliwoha and turned south off the road.

We did stop briefly in Eliwoha to pick up an *aban* as our guide and to show us the traditional migration route down to the Chelaka River. The spot we were aiming for wasn't actually in Abu Sama'ara territory, but their people regularly took herds down there to water in high summer and it was easy enough to find a man who was familiar with the route and knew who we would have to talk to in order to get permission for our survey.

As we moved southward, the countryside became more rolling, with small hills and a much denser covering of camel thorn bushes and other scrub. There were also a few more of the large acacia trees, not all of them situated beside defunct water courses. There were no roads and the few tracks we crossed were more suitable for goats than Land Rovers, so travel was necessarily slow. We pushed our way through virgin bush for almost four hours, with thorn bushes scraping and scratching along the sides of the vehicle. These bushes are heavily armed with barbed hooks or straight two-inch thorns, strong enough to pierce leather; strong enough to be used by the Afar to make awls for sewing their goat skin sandals.

Within two hours we had had three punctures. I blessed Elamu for insisting that we bring at least four spares. He would have his work cut out mending the other three when we eventually stopped.

When the third tyre blew, we were on a small ridge. Below us we could see the valley of the Chelaka River, marked out by a line of greenery where the tops of large trees growing along the bank betrayed its course. This view was very different from the sea of grey thorn scrub we had observed from previous ridges but, despite the line of greenery, it still looked very arid.

Our *aban* now decided that he didn't want to go any further. He had shown us the way to the Chelaka and he wanted to go back to Eliwoha. We said he had promised to introduce us to the man we needed to consult for permission to survey, but he refuted this. He said he had only agreed to tell us who to talk to and gave us the man's mane. No amount of cajolery would persuade him to stay and, after an hour of haggling, it was clear that all we could do was pay him his agreed fee and let him go.

We had put the kettle on when we stopped so we gave him a tin of sickly sweet tea along with his wages, told him to keep the tin, and left him squatting on the ridge as we drove down into the valley.

LUCK WAS WITH US as we found a suitable campsite in the first few minutes. It was situated just below a sharp bend in the river. Upstream of this there were natural rock outcrops that might form a good base for a barrage. There was lots of loose stone in the river bed and a broad flat pan on the bank a few hundred yards downstream looked ideal for making field basins. The only disadvantage appeared to be that the area where the fields would be was covered with particularly dense thorn scrub and a few large trees. It would not only be a major task to clear the scrub for cultivation, it would make surveying the land particularly tricky and time-consuming.

First, however, we needed to find the local *makaban* and get permission to survey. We had no idea where he might be. Mohamed suggested we should walk down the river until we found someone watering their animals. We could then ask them where to find the *makaban*. It sounded like good sense and a simple solution but the reality of achieving it was far from easy.

The dense scrub made following the river in the Land Rover completely impossible. The only practical way of going downstream was to walk in the dry river bed. This meant leaving the vehicle unattended which was an invitation for anyone passing to help themselves to the contents, but who should stay behind? Elamu was not willing to stay on his own and we couldn't leave Mohamed as we needed him to speak to the Afar when we found them. We discussed it for half an hour over the inevitable cup of tea, brewed using fresh water from the stream, and finally decided that Mohamed and I would walk downstream and try to find someone, while Bruce and Elamu would stay with the vehicle and make camp. We would aim to be back before sunset, even if we hadn't found anyone.

We must have walked about six miles down that river bed before we met a young man of about sixteen, watering a small herd of goats at a shady pool. He looked alarmed as we approached and tried to gather his goats and make off into the scrub before we got too close. In the end we had a shouted conversation with him from about fifty yards away.

Mohamed explained that we were looking for the *makaban*. The boy told us he was a full day's walk away from there and indicated the direction in which his camp lay. He named the piece of ground but, not being familiar with the area, the name meant nothing to us. Finally Mohamed asked him to send word to the *makaban* to tell him where we were camped and to say that we would come to see him in a few days. As payment for this service we offered him some cigarettes and a small bag of sugar which we placed in a prominent position on a rock before we withdrew. When we were about a hundred yards away we turned and saw the lad scramble over the rocks and collect his booty. We had left a box of matches with the cigarettes and were not surprised to see a small puff of blue smoke as he lit the first one.

The boy returned to his goats and a few minutes later he drove them across the stream to our side and melted into the scrub. We turned and started the long walk back upstream.

It was almost dusk by the time we reached camp. Bruce and Elamu had put up a fly sheet and were busy cooking rice to go with our supper. Over the meal we agreed that the simplest thing was to start the survey and then stop and talk if the *makaban* or any of his henchmen who turned up wanting to discuss it. If nobody came, we would finish the job and then try to find the *makaban* on our return journey northward. We could then explain what we had been doing in his territory and what might come of it.

We were woken early the next morning by a troop of baboons barking on the far side of the river. There were about fifteen of them scampering about on the rocks and a few others down by the stream, drinking. They had their own sentries on watch, seated on prominent stones nearby while the others drank. We in turn kept an eye on them and tried not to attract their attention while we made breakfast and got our surveying equipment ready. After about half an hour the troop moved off downstream. We were sure they were aware of our presence and wondered why these normally inquisitive animals had ignored us. It couldn't have been because they were on the other side of the river because the stream here was a mere trickle, barely more than a yard wide and no more than ankle-deep. By the way some of them had been playing in the water, they were not afraid of getting wet.

Since the most difficult part of the task was going to be surveying the field area, we started with that and set up a datum point beside our camp. Using a compass and a tape measure to locate the staff positions, we surveyed outwards in a series of lines from this point. Unfortunately it wasn't possible to see more

Bruce surveying. Dense bush added to the job's difficulty.

than about twenty yards and this meant that the level and the sighting staff had to be moved very frequently. It made the task much more complicated than it should have been and slowed the whole process down, but we gradually built up a grid and it looked as if four or five days would be enough time to prove the site's viability. As we moved, I took soil samples from regular points across the grid. We tested these each day during the hottest period when it was impractical to use the level because the heat haze distorted the surveyor's view of the staff and made optical surveying impossible.

After we had made a topographical plan of the proposed field area, we took detailed measurements upstream where the weir would go and marked out a possible route for the take-off and channel. The top section of this, unfortunately, would pass through an outcrop of rock and might need blasting or drilling. Mohamed was becoming quite good at wielding the surveying staff, so while he helped Bruce with surveying the channel, I collected and tested more soil samples. We had reckoned it would take five days to survey and get a plan drawn; it took us eight.

ON THE LAST DAY we broke camp and headed back the way we had come. Our inbound track through the scrub was easy to see and within a couple of hours we were out of the scrub and into more open country. Once we could choose our direction more freely, we turned east in the hope of finding the place where the boy by the river had told us the *makaban* was camped. We drove for about three more hours before sighting two men with a small herd of goats and fat-tailed sheep.

The men stood in a familiar pose, each on one leg, leaning on their spears as they watched us approach. When we were about two hundred yards away, I asked Elamu to stop and Mohamed and I climbed down and went towards them on foot.

As we got closer they put their other feet on the ground and, almost in unison, transferred their spears to their left hands.

"Good," Mohamed said. "They are not getting ready to fight."

"How do you know?"

"They do not shake hands with the left hand. A weapon is always held in the right to use it," he said and made me feel slightly foolish for not having known this. I realised there was a lot I had to learn about the Afar.

Our luck was in; these men were friendly and told us the *makaban* we were looking for was camped not far away. They would be pleased to show us the way. Afar men tend to be insatiably curious about everyone else's business and these were no exception, asking many questions about who we were and why we were there. I left Mohamed to answer them as he had shown himself to be good at explaining our mission and, as a foreigner himself, coming from a northern tribe, he was as interested as we were in the success of our negotiations. Apart from any working considerations, our own safety could depend on the outcome of these discussions.

Close by was obviously a relative term as it took more than three hours walking to reach the *makaban*'s camp. That was partly because the two Afar were driving animals ahead of them and partly because it was actually quite a long way. Time and distance, I realised, have different meanings here. It was as well to reckon everything would be twice or three times as far away as people said and it would take at least double the time they suggested to do anything or to go anywhere. Lessons were coming thick and fast.

The *makaban*, when we eventually met him, turned out to be a wiry individual called Has'same. He was about forty years old but looked seventy, with a wrinkled skin that appeared to be two sizes too big for him. He had knobbly, arthritic fingers and winced if his hand was gripped too firmly when greeted. He seemed, however, to be friendly enough and had already heard all about what we were doing down by the Chelaka. The Afar had evidently had spies watching us, although we had seen nobody except an old man and the boy Mohamed and I had encountered watering his goats. But the *makaban*'s information was good and far more detailed than either the old man or the boy would have been able to give him.

In addition, Has'same understood the principles of irrigation. He had been to Dubti and seen the vast irrigated farm there. While he realised that what we were proposing would be a lot smaller, he at least had the right idea, which would help when it came to explaining to his clansmen. Things looked promising and I was hopeful that we would have a positive negotiation when we came back to discuss actual work. We explained that our visit this time was only to see if anything was feasible and that we would be back later to talk to him and the elders in more detail, once we had looked at some other places and made proper plans. At that time we would explain everything to anyone who was interested.

Has'same said he was satisfied with this. He accepted a small gift of sugar and flour and gave us an *aban* to ensure our safe passage through his territory as far as the road. The guide didn't have a clue what sort of terrain a Land Rover is capable of crossing and took us by a very roundabout route. It was presumably one that suited grazing animals and eventually delivered us onto the road in the middle of nowhere, in countryside none of us recognised. He was adamant that Weranzo, the village we were aiming for, was only a short walk to the east, but we weren't convinced.

After the guide left us we got the sextant out and plotted our position. It was late in the day and the sun angle was low, but the reading still suggested that Weranzo lay more than twenty miles in the opposite direction. Trusting our own readings, we turned left and headed towards the dim grey line of mountains which showed low on the horizon, about a hundred miles away. The road here was in good condition and we made good time. Twenty-two miles later we came to Weranzo and stopped at Fred's bar for a beer.

The village policemen both sauntered over to see who had arrived and we asked them where we might find the Dodha *makaban*. It turned out that he not only lived in the village, but that he was at home at the time. Mohamed went off to speak to him and ask if he would talk to us. He returned a few minutes later with a smart looking man in his late thirties dressed in a light flowery sarong and a brown short-sleeved shirt. This was Doga Detolali. The Dodha *makaban* proved to be an affable and educated man and it didn't take long for us to discover that he spoke Amharic as well as Afar and that he could read and write in both languages. Afar is not normally considered a written language but both he and Mohamed assured us that it was sometimes written in Arabic script, particularly in the shared territory of Djibouti.

The mention of Djibouti prompted me to ask if he understood any French and we were pleased to discover that he had a passable understanding of that language as well. This made things a lot simpler as it meant I would be able to talk to him directly, without needing an interpreter. It wouldn't put Mohamed out of a job because we still needed him to translate for everyone else, but it gave me another window through which to acquire a working knowledge of the language myself and possibly to explore questions which I preferred, at least in the early stages, not to broadcast through open translation.

Doga was certainly a prosperous man and it soon emerged that he was quite widely travelled. He was one of the very few Afar I met who had made the Haj pilgrimage to Mecca. Although nominally Muslim, few Afar among the southern tribes appeared to take it particularly seriously. Doga told me that down in Assayita, where the Afar Sultan lived, the religion was stronger, but here among the people of the open desert it didn't have much relevance. This was confirmed when he accepted the beer Bruce offered him as we sat talking round the rickety table in Fred's bar.

Doga stayed and ate spaghetti with us that evening, along with two of the other tribal leaders who happened to be in the village at the time. One was Farasabba Mohamed, one of the oldest men in the tribe and also a *dagnya* or elder. He was a tall man with hawk-like features who seldom smiled beyond his eyes, but whose mind was a storehouse of tribal knowledge and accumulated wisdom. We worked out that he must have been more than sixty-five years old, which was exceptional among these people. The other man was called Alibi. By his features he appeared to be related to Doga but, unlike the *makaban*, he said little and seemed lost in thought much of the time. I realised later that he was listening very carefully for whenever he did say something it was always particularly pertinent and picked up on points everyone else had overlooked.

That evening we explained once more why we were there and what our mission was supposed to achieve. We told them about

*The makaban and heir: Doga Detolali and his
three and a half year old, Amir.*

the location we had found about ten miles north of the village and
asked if we might take them there and explain what the work
would involve. We thought it might make more sense to them
when they saw it on the ground. After several hours of discussion,
Doga and the others left us, saying they would meet us at the place
we had described the following morning. We offered to take them
in the Land Rover but they declined, saying they would walk and
bring others along too.

It had been dark for some time by this stage, so we drove a few

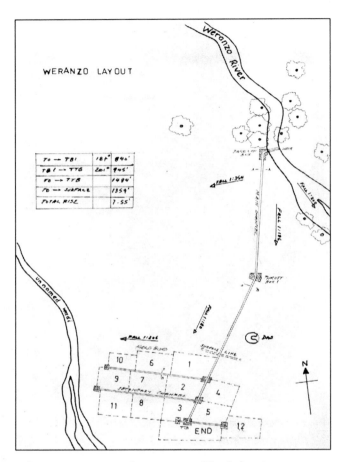

The more we saw, the more we liked the site.

miles along the tracks left by our last visit and camped under a clump of large tamarisk trees. We didn't bother making a full camp, but the four of us spent half an hour constructing a rough thorn fence round the parked Land Rover and fly sheet tent before we stretched out on our camp beds and slept soundly.

We were up with the rising sun, made coffee and packed up all our gear. Then we drove up the twin lines of our old tyre tracks towards the bend in the *wadi* where we proposed constructing the irrigation project. We had already decided that this site would be the first to see any work because there were more people in this area. In addition, the responses we had received from those we had spoken to had been positive and the ground lent itself to the work without undue complications.

We arrived before any of the Afar and decided to run a few transit lines to verify the rough information we collected last time. So we banged in a stout post with a nail beaten flush into the top to serve as a datum point and took levels over about four hundred yards south-eastwards as well as across the dry river bed. After that we walked over a wide area, collecting soil samples and generally having a good look at the land. The more we saw, the more we liked it. By the time the first Afar showed up, Bruce had drawn a rough plan on a large sheet of paper, showing the shape of the river channel, a weir across the dry river bed, a channel from one side of the weir, snaking its way across the countryside and then an area of square fields where we hoped to grow food.

While Bruce and I were taking the last measurements, Elamu and Mohamed put up two large fly sheets to form a huge awning. Although there were several big acacia trees near the river bank, there was almost no shade during the middle of the day, so the awning would provide a comfortable place to sit and talk if anyone came.

The Afar arrived just before midday, twenty or more men, all dressed in traditional bright white clothes, festooned with large *gillés* and with their distinctive aroma of rancid butter. About half of them had rifles and everyone else had a spear or a long stick with iron wound round one end of it. Noticing the absence of women, I wondered if they ever had any say in tribal discussions, or if this was a uniquely male preserve. It wasn't, as I later discovered.

We already had a kettle cooking to make tea and had been saving empty food tins throughout our trip, knowing that it might be advantageous to distribute tea freely when there was talking to be done. Elamu counted heads and found we had just enough empty tins for the crowd who turned up.

The talking went on all afternoon without reaching any definite conclusion, but things looked positive. As sunset approached the Afar stood up and took their leave, saying we would continue the discussion in the morning. As they left, we noticed a number of them looking with interest at a line of red and white surveying poles which we had left scattered across the nearby countryside, marking out the probable route of the main channel. We wondered if someone might take a fancy to one, but they were all still there in the morning. This surprised us as each pole was fitted with a well-made conical spike at its tip and they made excellent javelins if one chose to throw them. Given the Afar's love of spears, some of them must have been sorely tempted to walk off with one. The red and white paint would be easy enough to scrape off.

The tribesmen returned early the following morning and the talking began again. There were some new faces this time and we had to go over everything that had already been said at least twice, until all who wanted to ask questions had asked them and all who wanted to make comments had had their say. Even though much of the time was spent repeating things, a pattern emerged in the way they did this and I soon realised that it didn't matter if someone had already said something, every man was entitled to his say and if he wanted to repeat what someone else had already said, then everyone listened politely until he was finished.

This was to become another familiar feature of Afar negotiations. It was a lesson in patience because however much you tried to hurry them on, they would always come back until everyone present had had their say and asked their questions.

By the end of the second day, I thought we were nearly done. Then a man who had arrived late asked what all the coloured poles were for and insisted on being taken round and having the significance of each and every one explained. I ducked at this and asked Bruce to do it. He was the engineer and surveyor and would explain far better than I could why he had put poles in particular places. The rest of us just followed and listened.

For nearly an hour this went on and as we neared the end of the line I realised that we had a problem. The last but one pole was situated near a slight mound. Closer inspection of the ground showed that this mound was horseshoe shaped, with a slight dip at its centre. It turned out to be a *das* and, as such, was a significant feature in the landscape.

The mound was barely a foot above the general level of the surrounding ground and the depression in the middle was no more than a few inches deep. It was an ancient burial site. Nobody knew who had been buried there, or when, but the *das* had a name, which everybody knew, and it could not be despoiled in any way by digging. In fact, the man told us, we should not dig within about thirty yards of it.

Later on I saw many such mounds and learned to recognise them at a glance as *wadella*, the local generic name for these monuments. This one must have been very ancient as it had been badly eroded and was barely discernable, but others were prominent and many had stone horseshoe structures around them. It was an old style of grave which must have involved considerable work to construct as there was seldom any stone nearby. I was to see many more modern graves in the months ahead and even had to help build some of them when disease ripped through the community and left the people unable to bury their own dead.

The more modern ones were less complicated, amounting to little more than a conical mound of stones, but they still required a lot of heavy work to construct. Given the starvation and weak condition of the people, this was a considerable task.

We went back to the awning, brewed more tea and talked about the significance of burial sites. In the end it was accepted that when we laid out our site we would take particular care to keep well away from this *das*. I didn't dare ask if there were any other mounds of this sort in the area in case someone else knew of one and I could imagine the whole plan unravelling before my eyes. But nobody else raised the possibility and we eventually shook hands on a deal.

There would, of course, have to be more negotiations before construction work started, to determine which clans would work as well as when and how each would benefit from anything it finally produced. In any case, the Dodha was one of the larger tribes and three of its clans had not been represented in this group. They would have to be consulted and give their agreement before we did anything more than survey.

A deal was clearly always conditional and not really a deal until long after it was delivered. Even then, I suspected, there might be reservations, but it seemed that since they were so thorough in their consideration they might keep their word when it was given. A promise was evidently a serious commitment. As I learned later, all this talking and agreement did include women and children, all of whom were heard with equal attention. Negotiating with the Afar may be a long-winded and convoluted process, but at least when they made a deal, everybody was more or less in agreement with it.

FOR THE NEXT TWO DAYS we ran detailed transit lines, noting the levels on a fifty-yard grid, right down to the end of the field area. We realigned the channel to avoid the ancient burial site and drew a detailed topographical plan. All the time we were watched by a number of the men who had participated in the discussions, but they never tried to impede us, to get in the way or to delay what we were doing by asking more questions. That would surely come later. For now they just stood around and watched.

By the time the survey was complete, we realised time was getting short and we needed to move on. The Uua River was too far north to cover in this trip. Given the experience we had already had trying to reach the place, it also imposed major logistical problems for any work that might one day be carried out there. If this scheme proved its worth, it might be possible to do something there in the future.

For now, however, our objective was to get down to the Jeldi Plain and have a look at that. This meant we needed to go back to Eliwoha and find the Abu Sama'ara *makaban*.

We stopped at Fred's bar in Weranzo to further deplete his dwindling stock of beer and to warn him to stock up as we would be back. If nothing else, out project was going to make an impact on the economy of this dishevelled little hamlet. We called on Doga Detolali, thanked him for his help and told the policemen where we were going. I also enquired what was necessary for them to start distributing some of the grain still stacked in a pyramid beside their police post. They told me they would need a direct order from the District Governor. That was not going to be easy for us to obtain with him already upset by our having defied him over the armed escort. He was unlikely to take kindly to any suggestion that he might actually save a few lives by distributing the stockpiled food. Maybe we'd have to go further up the chain and get instructions from provincial level.

We set out for Eliwoha, pausing to take a surreptitious look at the Jeldi Plain on our way past. There were a number of locations where we could install very small dams to block minor ravines in the foothills of an old caldera, but beyond that there was only one large site. Any possibility of exploiting this for an irrigated site would depend on the way the ground sloped and the difference in levels. Without a detailed topographical survey, there was no way of guessing whether it was viable or not. To do the survey we needed the *makaban*'s and probably the *balabat*'s permission.

The *makaban* still wasn't back in Eliwoha and nobody among the few Afar hanging around the village had any idea when he would be back. They declined even to talk about the *balabat*. When we asked about him we soon realised that, because he was a government appointee and not one of their traditional *dagnyas*, he had neither respect nor authority in the tribe. We had been told as part of the briefing in Addis Ababa that everything we did would have to be sanctioned by the local *balabats*, so this was something else to sort out later. Everything we heard about the two men made it seem quite likely that the *makaban* and the *balabat* would necessarily not agree with one another when it came to decision time.

Getting permission from the Abu Sama'ara *makaban* looked like being a problem. The man had a less amenable reputation than the Dodha leader so, in view of his continued absence, we decided to call it a day and head back to Bati. We had plenty of work to get on with planning the Weranzo operation, working out what tools would be needed and writing a project schedule.

We also needed to make sure there would be adequate supplies of food that the Afar could eat. This had to be under our control to be distributed as payment for work done; assuring the continuity of supply would be vital.

In addition, Bruce and I both felt the desert people had to receive usable relief supplies without further delay so that there might be a few still alive and capable of work when we were ready to start. This meant a whole new game of negotiation, with the government officials this time, and the various relief agencies that controlled supplies.

I hoped we might have all this sorted out in the next few weeks, before Bruce returned to England, but if not I had my trump card ready to play – the director, Anna Greening, always assuming she turned up.

THERE WAS STILL no sign of the District Governor when we got back to Bati and Ato Hapteab was unable to tell us anything about when he might be back. I spent a day going round the international relief agencies working at the big camp on the edge of the town to see if I could persuade any of them to send some help down the main road to the Afar. But they were all at full stretch and logistics was always a problem. Starving drought-stricken people were still arriving at their camp at the rate of more than two thousand every day and the death rate was nearly half that. Most of those dying were either the very young or the very old; about half died from the effects of long-term malnutrition.

Others, brought to this desperate state by the drought, were mere skeletons wrapped in paper-thin skin and would not have looked out of place in those films I had seen of survivors of the concentration camps at Belsen and Buchenwald at the end of the Second World War. Many died of virulent diseases which were now beginning to spread because of the sheer number of people and the unsanitary conditions in the camp. The relief teams did their best to provide clean water and sanitation but with such a mass of humanity all crammed together and disease already rampant, it was an uphill struggle which held little hope for many of its victims.

Cholera, along with a variety of fevers and the most virulent, dysentery, had recently raised its ugly head. All of these diseases imposed impossible burdens on an already overloaded system and the relief teams were all at their wits' end trying to cope.

I stopped what I was supposed to be doing for two days and helped dig new latrine pits at the Bati camp, aware that this was but one of a number of such places along the eastern escarpment. The drought extended to communities as far north as Mekele in Tigray province.

Later I helped lay pipes to bring fresh water from a large cistern to a series of standpipes around the camp. Enabling people to come and fill their water containers without having to trek across the camp to a central point helped make infection control possible. Each of the standpipes was fitted with a valve which dispensed only two gallons at a time, ensuring that the water could be rationed and more people got a share.

With all this going on, there was no help to spare for the Afar.

8 ~ Interim

WITH TWO DETAILED SURVEYS completed and preliminary plans drawn for the Weranzo system, Bruce went home at the end of his appointed stay and I found myself on my own with a delay of a few weeks before the main project started. This came about because the Ethiopian government decided it did not want a white foreigner working down in the Danakil alone. Unable to persuade one of their own men to take on the task, they had asked HMG for another person to be sent out from UK. Their request was for a civil engineer with earth-moving experience and some knowledge of irrigation ditches and building weirs by the method we had chosen.

Government wheels grind slowly at times like this and someone had yet to be appointed. I was therefore at a loose end for a few weeks and able to spend some time on my other task, but the date on which I hoped our director would come was fast approaching, so I was not short of something to do.

As well as drawing plans for the Weranzo project, Bruce and I had compiled detailed lists of the tools and equipment that would be needed. After consulting some of the doctors at the Bati relief camp, I had worked out types and quantities of food we would require to pay the Afar for their labour once work started. I also needed to feed them properly until then so that they would be capable of work when they were needed.

After seeing Bruce's plane depart, I took the plans and lists back to Bati. It would make more sense to source the tools from local markets and, since I now had funds to buy them, it was an opportunity to do this without other pressures or meddling from the LMB officials in their head office. I spent two days patrolling the local hardware suppliers in Bati, Dessie and Kombolcha and loaded the Land Rover with great piles of tools. These had no handles, but I reasoned that if I made a few as examples, it would be a constructive way of introducing the Afar to using tools by getting them to make the rest from the acacia scrub we would have to clear from the site. They were accustomed to harvesting these bushes for their sticks and spears and for making stock enclosures to keep their herds safe at night, so it was only a small step to select slightly thicker stems and fit them to shovels, rakes and hoes.

It would be a different matter teaching them how to use the new tools and getting them to work accurately. These people had no history or culture of this kind of work, having spent the last thousand years as pastoralists, following their cattle's tails from one grazing area to another, so this was going to be a new to experience for them.

Among the tools I bought were fifty good machetes for cutting the acacia sticks, although I suspected that when it came to it the Afar would probably prefer to use their own *gillés*. These were heavy enough for the task and had the benefit that the men already had them and were proficient at wielding them.

I also bought a five-hundred gallon tank mounted on a trailer which could be towed behind the Land Rover. It would be important for providing drinking water on the work site. I intended to fill this from a well near the worksite which I would dig where I had found an underground reservoir about fifteen feet below the nearby river bed. It was located in a spot not normally used by the Afar as a water source and I hoped that my ability to find and access water like this might impress the people at least a little and persuade them that we foreigners did know what we were talking about. In the early stages of a project like this, creating that sort of belief among the people who will benefit is essential if they are to agree the plan and commit to working on it.

Bruce had suggested that a model of the system might be helpful to show how it worked when explaining things to the rest of the Afar. So I spent a day with sand and cement making mud pies and creating a mini irrigation system on a large board. This had a river channel, shaped like the Weranzo River at the point where the weir would go. The weir itself was represented by small pebbles wrapped in wire mesh and laid across the river bed as a barrier. A long groove from one end of the barrier led diagonally across the board to square basins at the far end. By pouring water in at the top people could watch it being diverted to the side by the weir, flowing down the channel and into the fields. I would encourage them to get involved and pour the water in themselves and hoped this would help them understand and make explanation of the idea much easier.

With the inside of the vehicle full of tools and supplies, Elamu and I tied the model onto the Land Rover's roof rack and headed for the desert. I intended to make camp in the tamarisk grove again and then employ a local man to keep an eye on it. The grove would make a good base camp as it was within easy reach of the village and the worksite and it would only be a short trip each day to get to work. The trees offered a little protection from the hot desert winds, even if they didn't actually give much shade.

Mohamed had joined us in Bati as we came through and so he, Elamu and I spent an afternoon putting up two tents, cutting enough thorn bushes to make a good fence around the camp and establishing ourselves. There was a small cluster of the domed Afar *a'aris* nearby where three families had camped and one of their lads, a boy called Mula, agreed to be our camp guardian.

Once we were settled, I spent as much time as I could among the Afar, trying to learn more of the language. In this Mohamed was quite helpful and I began noting down all the words and phrases I learned. The Afar found my efforts amusing, and I noticed that as the days passed there was a slight relaxation in their manner. They were still wary of outsiders, but at least the majority of them seemed friendly and thoughts of the brutal way they were reputed to deal with strangers had long ago slipped from my mind.

With our camp established, Elamu, Mohamed and I spent two hours each day cutting straight acacia branches to make handles for shovels, rakes and hoes. This activity provoked a lot of curiosity among the Afar. Whenever we sat down to trim the thorns off our harvest and shape the sticks to fit the tools, it invariably attracted an audience of curious men. After a while I offered a stick and a shovel head to one of them and invited him to try and make a handle. He proved much more dextrous than me at removing the thorns, but had difficulty shaping the end of the stick so that it fitted tightly in the shaft of the shovel. But it didn't take him long to learn once he understood why the tightness was important. A few attempts later and after seeing his shovel head fall off when I tried to dig with it, he got the idea.

Over the next few days, encouraged by the offer of sweet tea and food, a few more men joined in and we soon had a production line going. It was very slow and, to start with, at least half of their handles had to be remade, but at least they were trying.

Once we had a supply of tools, I began to dig the well. It was situated about fifty yards from another river bank, a few hundred yards to the west of the camp. The ground was firm and not prone to collapse and I made rapid progress. While I went down the hole and dug, Mohamed stood on the surface and pulled up buckets of spoil. It was too hot to work during the middle part of the day, but by starting at dawn and working for about three and a half hours and then doing a similar stint in the late afternoon, I was able to get down to fifteen feet in only a few days and soon found the soil becoming markedly damper. After that it only took another day to dig into the aquifer.

While Mohamed and I had been working on the well, Elamu had walked up and down the river bed selecting flat stones and

Soon we had a production line making tool handles.

piling them up nearby. A few of the Afar women, understanding what he wanted and realising that they would be given food if they helped, joined in and the pile grew rapidly. By the time the digging was done and we had clear water in the bottom of the hole there was enough stone stockpiled to build a good strong lining the full depth of the well, with steps in the wall to enable people to descend or climb out easily.

With the lining installed, I built a *shaduf* to make going to the bottom largely unnecessary as water could simply be lifted to the surface by a counter-balanced arm. It was a little too deep to be really effective, but it looked impressive and made raising water a great deal easier than pulling up yards of rope with a bucket on the end. The last thing I did was to build a strong thorn fence round the top of the well to stop animals trampling it down and polluting the clean water. This seemed to be a completely new idea to the Afar. They were accustomed to walking their animals right down and into the water to drink. It might have been less work for them but the water soon got fouled, while my method kept it clean and sweet for everyone to drink, animal and human alike.

9 ~ The director feels the heat

IT WAS SIX WEEKS since I had arrived and an important date was fast approaching. If she stuck to our bargain, I was about to have a visitor from London. Leaving Mohamed and Elamu to finish the camp enclosure fence and make a few more handles, I took the Land Rover and went back up to Addis Ababa to meet the plane. I intended to be back the following day and, as Elamu had slowly become accustomed to being among the Afar and was losing his in-bred fear of them, he was willing to let me go on my own.

Sitting at the airport, waiting for the London flight to arrive, I looked around to see if any of the staff from the British Embassy were also waiting for this flight. It was almost certain that, if she did come, they would have been warned and would be there in force to meet her, despite my request for no razzmatazz. But there was nobody who looked remotely British.

The flight arrived and after about fifteen minutes, passengers began to stream into the arrivals lounge. I watched them from the glazed spectators' gallery. There was no sign of my painted lady anywhere but, in case I had just missed seeing her in the crowd, I decided to wait outside the exit from the customs hall until all the passengers had emerged before abandoning my quest, so I settled myself against a pillar to watch the door.

To my surprise, I didn't have long to wait for she emerged at the front of the crowd, saw me waiting and came straight over.

"Did you think I'd let you down?" she asked by way of greeting.

"I did wonder," I admitted, taking her bag and leading the way out to the car park.

"The grey man persuaded me not to," she said. "In fact if he told me once he told me a dozen times they couldn't afford for you to walk out and I had given my word, so here I am. So, what have you got in store for me?"

"We'll go up to Wollo this afternoon and stop in Dessie overnight," I explained. "That's the provincial capital where about half the relief effort control is located. We'll do a quick tour of the agencies in the morning before we go down to Bati. There I'll take you for a brief look at the big relief camp on the edge of town. I hope you have a strong stomach. It's pretty unpleasant but you can see at first hand the pictures you've been getting on your television. We'll go down to the desert tomorrow afternoon and there I'll show you the project and introduce you to the Afar."

We had reached the car park by this time and I noticed the slight look of dismay on Anna's face as we approached the dusty Land Rover. We may have been up in the mountains but it was standing in full sun and the wave of heat as I opened the door gave a clear impression of what she was in for.

"I hope you've got some very light clothes," I said. "It gets bloody hot down in the desert and you'll be going from fourteen thousand feet up in the mountains at Dessie down to three hundred feet below sea level when we get to Weranzo."

"I can cope with the heat," she said.

"A hundred and forty-eight degrees Fahrenheit and near zero humidity?"

"Oh! Yes, that is hot."

AS WE DROVE UP the long and winding road towards Debre Berhan, I explained what had been done so far and how I intended to proceed once the new engineer arrived. She told me recruitment was proving a little less than easy and some of the major civil engineering companies had now been approached to see if they would second someone.

We stopped in Debre Berhan at my favourite café and I ordered two portions of *injera* and *wat* for a late lunch. Anna looked at it dubiously. "What is it?" she asked.

"*Injera wat*," I said, "literally bread and stew. This is the staple food here in the mountains. It's quite good once you get over the psychological shock of how it looks."

"It looks like a sheet of Sorbo rubber with a pile of shit in the middle," she said, watching me tear off a long strip of *injera* and dunk it in the sauce.

"It probably tastes like it too," I said, enjoying her discomfort. "But it keeps you alive." I stuffed my mouth and started chewing.

She watched for several minutes and then took a small piece herself and dipped it in the sauce. Her face betrayed that she hadn't expected all the chilli, but she persisted and ate the whole mouthful, gulping at the water that the proprietor brought in a cracked glass jug, despite the apparent insanitary state of the glasses. By the time she had finished, she'd eaten more than half what she had been given.

We arrived in Dessie soon after dark, checked into a small

hotel and slept soundly. At least, I did. I was exhausted after driving all the way up to Addis from the desert and most of the way back. I had been behind the wheel for almost twenty hours.

After breakfast the next morning, we went to the market where I bought a selection of baggy tee shirts and a few lengths of brightly coloured cotton cloth in which to wrap my guest, reasoning that her western garb would be most unsuitable where we were going. Anna bridled at my suggestion she should abandon her bra and simply wear a tee shirt with a length of cloth wrapped round as a long skirt, until I told her that the Afar women would be naked to the waist and nobody was going to be interested in her boobs. The tee shirts were only to stop them getting sunburned.

The visit to the Bati relief camp was a shock. We arrived as the triage team was dealing with a group of nearly a thousand new arrivals. Among them were four babies who had the look of death about them. One of them died as we watched, while her mother was waiting patiently in line. When she realised the child was dead, the mother simply wrapped it in the cloth she had been using to carry it, laid the bundle on the ground at her feet and continued to wait, her face bereft of all expression or sign of hope.

Anna was quiet and thoughtful as we left Bati and started down the winding road towards the desert. She didn't utter a word until we stopped at the spring to top up our water bottles.

Our arrival on the desert floor coincided with the hottest part of the day. The draught through the open windows and dash board scuttles was a searing hot blast and the shimmering heat haze reflected from the flat land reduced visibility to just over a hundred yards. Into this inferno we drove, the relentless sun boring straight down on us. An hour and a half later, we reached

Elamu and Mohamed set up a new tent for our visitor.

Weranzo and stopped at Fred's bar. There we found Mohamed and Elamu resting in the shade. They had walked into the village early that morning. We stopped only long enough to swallow a cold beer before going on to our camp under the tamarisk trees.

While I had been away, they had put up another tent for our visitor. They had also stockpiled some fallen branches from the trees and made a fireplace out of flat stones. The camp was tidy and almost homely as I settled our guest into her new accommodation and suggested she should have a siesta while I caught up with what had been going on. I left her to rest in her tent and took Mohamed up to the worksite to inspect the tool handles that had been made in my absence. I wanted time to talk to him alone.

When we got back, we found Elamu making tea and Anna trying to talk to him and finding his accent difficult to understand. She had changed, adopting the attire I bought her in Dessie. We spent the rest of the afternoon going over the project plans, explaining about the negotiations that had taken place so far and what it would be necessary to agree with the Afar before work could begin. She found this shocking, having never considered the minutiae of how projects like this worked and were actually implemented. I also told her about the problems we had encountered with the District Governor in Bati. She had seen the pyramid of grain in Weranzo which we had passed on our way through and I explained what would be needed for our 'food-for-work' programme to succeed, suggesting that a written instruction from her might oil a few wheels and help us get what was required; after all, it was her department that was paying the bill.

As the afternoon waned, we walked across to the Afar encampment so that she could get a closer look at the way the people lived. I noticed her nose wrinkle at the aroma of the men and saw her face reflect her shock at the absolute poverty of their dwellings. She became thoughtful when I told her that from time to time the people would simply dismantle their *a'aris*, tying the sticks that made the frames into two bundles and rolling up the grass mats, load the whole lot onto a camel and wander off to set up house somewhere else, usually where there was more grazing or water for their sheep and goats.

Supper that night was corned beef hash, made with rice, a tin of corned beef, an onion and a few rather limp vegetables bought at the roadside in Bati. Whereas Mohamed, Elamu and I would normally have eaten out of the communal pot, I presented Anna her supper on a plate, thinking to introduce her slowly to the realities of bush living. After supper Mohamed made coffee which was thick with sludge, bitter as sin and only slightly improved by the pile of sugar he stirred into it until the spoon almost stood up on its own.

We sat and talked until about half past nine, watching the

brilliant stars and waiting for the thin crescent moon to rise. It didn't offer much more light, being only three days old, but it was bright enough for us to see the large hunting spiders dashing hither and thither across the ground in their nightly quest for food. These spiders have small bodies but their legs are up to two inches long and they travel remarkably fast. It is not unusual to feel a slight tickle as one passes over an unshod foot. This was too much for our guest, who chose to sit on an upturned wooden box and rest her feet on another until we all retired to our beds.

As I bid her goodnight, I couldn't resist the temptation to warn her about shaking out her shoes before putting them on if she should need to get up during the night.

"Why do I have to do that?" she asked.

"To shake out any scorpions or spiders before putting your foot in," I said. "Sleep well."

I HAD PLANNED to take Anna to look at the worksite early the next morning but my plans went awry in the middle of the night. In the small hours we were woken by a terrific racket coming from the Afar encampment. Some sort of altercation was in progress. Among the shouts, crashing pots and pans and shrill curses, there was vigorous bleating from penned sheep and goats punctuated by the occasional laughing whoop of a hyena. It appeared that one of these was trying to break into a stock pen, hoping to steal itself some supper, but the Afar were defending their animals with vigour.

Every few seconds I could hear the whizz of stones being launched into the darkness from slingshots as the men tried to drive off the marauder. After a few minutes everything settled down and peace and calm was restored. It had taken me a while to find my torch but now as I took it and went over to see what had happened, Mohamed materialised at my elbow.

The hyena had departed without its meal but not before it had inflicted a serious injury on the man whose animals it had been trying to kill. Giving no consideration to his own safety and thinking only of his livestock, he had launched himself at the animal with spear in hand and *gillé* drawn. Something of a tussle had ensued during which he had managed to injure the beast enough to make it withdraw. In its turn, however, the hyena had managed one good bite on his left arm and hand. This was now a mangled mess, dripping blood and in urgent need of attention.

Working alone in wild places, I always maintained an extensive first aid kit, capable of dealing with most emergencies of this sort, so I invited the man to come across to my camp where I would clean the wound and see what other attention it might need. Only with a decent light would we know how much damage had been done, but in the torchlight it looked bad. Leaving the rest of his family to make sure their animals were safe and the stock fence was secure against any renewed attack, the man came with me and sat down to wait while I lit a Tilley lamp. As soon as I could see what I was doing, I sorted out some morphine tablets for him to swallow to relieve the pain.

It did not take long for the morphine to take effect and then I was able to start cleaning the wound. Even with the analgesia it must have been excruciatingly painful, but the man neither flinched nor spoke; he just sat facing me with his injured hand resting on a white plastic sheet in my lap, watching as I flushed away the blood with a bag of sterile saline fluid and tried to identify what all the flapping bits of flesh were and where they belonged.

It was getting light by the time everything was clean. A

tourniquet round his arm had reduced the bleeding to mere seepage. Although the Tilley lamp had been reasonably bright, I was glad of the dawn light which let me see properly what I was doing as I tried to reassemble his arm and hand and sew them back together. I suspected the limb wouldn't be much use to him after this, but it had been important to try. With basic repairs done, I would take him up to Bati and ask one of the doctors in the relief camp to look at him. He could come with us when I took my guest back in a few days time. Until then it was make do and mend and hope he didn't get septicaemia; hyenas are unsanitary animals at the best of times and the likelihood of infection was high.

Soon after dawn, as I was stitching the muscles of his forearm back together, I was aware of a white arm appearing from the side and placing a plastic mug of tea on the ground beside my patient's right hand. A few moments later another was placed beside me. I hadn't realised how thirsty I was. The tea may have been sweet but it tasted like nectar. The man looked up and nodded his thanks, picked up the cup and drank, but otherwise remained motionless watching me sewing his flesh together.

Telling it like this, the whole episode sounds gruesome, but it wasn't as bad as it sounds. The tourniquet did a lot to reduce the gore and the man's pain must have been much reduced by the morphine as well as novocaine with which I generously infused the affected areas. Even so, I couldn't but admire his stoicism as he sat immobile and let me work.

At some point it dawned on me that I didn't even know his mane so I asked in Afar, "*Ku miga iya?*"

"Ahmed Djoun," was all he said, but he smiled as he replied.

"*Yi miga Ian,*" I told him my own name.

He smiled again and nodded.

It was necessary to tie off one major blood vessel and put more than 170 stitches in that arm and hand to make it look anything like it should. There was still a little movement in three of the fingers when I had finished and I hoped that if we could fend off infection he might have some limited use of these in the future. After washing everything again in disinfectant and dusting it with sulphanilamide powder, I wrapped the whole thing in gauze, bandaged it, and made a sling to support the arm. I told him I would look at it again in the evening. Meanwhile, if it began to hurt badly, or throb, he should tell me immediately and I would give him some more pain killers. Now he must lie and rest in the shade of our awning.

The sun was high by the time I had finished. I felt drained but there was still work to do. "Would you go and find out if any other Afar were injured," I asked Mohamed.

As I was cleaning the instruments I had been using, I was startled by a voice beside me asking in English, "Do you have to do that sort of thing often?"

I had completely forgotten our visitor.

"Occasionally," I said. "Most of the wounds are less dramatic. That one was a bit extreme, but I couldn't just do nothing."

"Where did you learn to do that? It looked very professional."

"I wish it were. I learned by facing situations just like that one and applying a basic knowledge of anatomy from school and numerous clinics and bush hospitals I've visited. The risk now is infection. I've covered it with antibiotic sulphur powder as you saw, but that won't work for long. We'll take him up to see a proper doctor when I take you back. Right now," I added, "I'm hungry and we have a worksite to look at. After that I want to show you some of the other problems that working here entails."

Before I could do any of that, however, Mohamed returned from the Afar encampment with another man called Djeni Dugama, who had also been injured by the hyena. During all the snapping and slashing he had been bitten on the calf. Examination showed it to be a relatively minor injury, but it still needed attention. I got the kit out again, cleaned his leg and put in three stitches to hold the wound closed. Once again I dusted it with antibiotic powder and bandaged the leg, telling Djeni that I wanted him to come with us when we took Ahmed to see the doctor in Bati.

As I packed up the first aid kit for the second time, Anna remarked that she felt sticky and dirty. "Were you telling me yesterday that you have a shower?" she asked.

"Yes," I said, "over there." I pointed to one of the tamarisk trees where a bucket hung above a rough hessian screen. "Ask Elamu for half a gallon of water and a sponge. That's how we do it here."

For a moment her face showed disbelief mixed with horror. Then, as she realised I was being serious, she gave me a venomous glare, as if I had concocted this discomfort especially for her benefit, and stalked off to get the bucket.

IT WAS ALMOST NOON before I took her to the worksite. We walked round with a set of plans in hand, explaining where the weir would be and how we were going to construct it. Then we followed the line of poles marking out the route of the main channel and I explained how a lesser gradient than the surrounding land would eventually bring the water to the surface when it reached an area where lines of small pegs, set out in large squares, showed the layout of future fields.

We inspected the tools and she watched some of the men making handles before I asked them to test those they had just made and show that the heads were securely fixed. It was obvious these men had no idea how to use the tools so I spent ten minutes showing them and making them try again. There was a lot of laughter and none of them moved much soil, but that would improve with practice. When Anna picked up a shovel and very neatly dug a short trench the laughter stopped. The idea that a woman could do this and they couldn't was a bit of a challenge. From then on they tried a bit harder.

People come out with the most interesting surprises and one never knows what they may be capable of. As we walked on, I asked where she acquired the ability to wield a spade with such proficiency. "Gardening jobs when I was a student," she said, "that and digging my own spuds."

I had never associated someone like her with gardening.

We went back to camp where I showed her the model and let her pour water into the top of the river channel. She seemed amused seeing it diverted by the weir and trickling down the long groove of the main channel. The simplicity of it pleased her and she began to understand something of what working with people like the Afar might be about.

Leaving the camp in Mula's care, we piled into the Land Rover with Mohamed and Elamu and set off to see some of the other Afar communities in the area. At one of these we were offered goat's milk in a smoked basket. Anna was surprised that a grass basket could be sufficiently watertight to hold liquid. She was fascinated to learn how it was done, by rubbing the inside of the basket with butter and then inverting it over a smoky fire for a few days to cure. I knew that the smoky taste of the milk was something she would never forget. Equally, it was not lost on her that, poor and starving though these people were, they had still shared their milk with us and she remarked on this. This hard-nosed woman did have feelings after all.

The heat was oppressive that afternoon and she wilted badly, finally spending three hours lying down in the shade of her tent with a bottle of water beside her. That evening she told me she had nearly ducked out of the trip. She'd been too embarrassed to admit to colleagues that I had blackmailed her so she'd taken some annual leave and not told anyone where she was going. 'Image is everything when you're in government,' I thought.

Now she began to ask intelligent questions about how I and the other field agents normally worked. We were only a small band, most of our government's effort being applied at a much higher lever, but she could see that a building without foundations wouldn't last long and our work at this base level was a necessary component. Seeing what we achieved with nothing made her appreciate how important the few facilities or pieces of equipment any of us asked for really were.

After another sweltering night, I took pity on her and we went back to the mountains. We took Ahmed Djoun and Djeni Dugama with us. They had prepared themselves for the trip and the smell of their newly dressed hair was even more pungent inside the hot Land Rover. At the relief camp, a German doctor who was working for a *Bundesgrenzschutz* relief team had a look at Ahmed's arm and gave him an injection of strong antibiotics. We asked Ahmed to stay at the camp for a few days so that the doctor could keep an eye on his arm. I would collect him on my return to Weranzo after going to Addis Ababa to drop off the director for her homeward flight. Djeni Dugama was similarly treated and when Mohamed offered to stay with them as a guarantee that I would return, they both agreed to remain at the camp. There were a few other Afar people in the camp by this stage, so I asked Mohamed to make himself useful and translate for the doctors to ensure that they got the attention they needed.

I TOOK ANNA to visit the District Governor at his office in the hope that her presence might defuse a bit of the wrath I expected after flagrantly ignoring his edicts. He was still away and nobody knew when he would return, so we left a note to say we had called and went off to see some of the other relief work being carried out by British agencies. A team of Royal Engineers had just arrived to construct roads and enable vehicular access to some of the more remote communities, so we called on them. Their invitation to stay for supper was music to my guest's ears and they fed us a slap-up, three-course army meal. After the heat and privations of my desert camp, and the indescribable experience of the *injera* which I had inflicted on her the day she arrived, Anna clearly enjoyed this visit.

The following day we drove back up to Addis Ababa. I took advantage of having her full attention to explain what was needed to implement the 'food-for-work' component of our programme. This required organisation on the ground which I would have neither the time nor the opportunity to accomplish while based down in the desert. After some consideration, she asked if it would be possible to visit the Embassy when we got to Addis. The development attaché resident there belonged to her department and would be charged with making the logistical arrangements and paying for the food, so it made sense to involve her at this point. The only snag might be that nobody at the Embassy had been told of her visit and it would come as something of a surprise for them when she turned up unannounced.

Getting her to visit in the way I had might have given me the benefit of her undivided attention for a few days, but it was unlikely to do anything for my popularity stakes with the diplomatic corps. There had already been several difficult interviews with the development attaché, who I found touchy, hostile and unhelpful. Until now I had thought this was because I was not answerable to her for my actions, but this was not going to improve our relationship. We were never destined to be soul mates because minor diplomats like her tend to love their petty empires and defend them as though they were sacred territory.

Show me a sacred cow and I'll show you a target.

Predictably the Embassy staff were surprised, outraged and finally scandalised when, after our visit, I took the director off to a small hotel in the market area rather than letting her stay at the Embassy or at one of the big international hotels in the city centre. I wanted her to myself for a few more hours before the flight home to make sure she fully understood how our team lived and worked. That was, after all, the real purpose of her visit as far as I was concerned.

The following morning, when I drove Anna out to the airport, five members of the Embassy staff were waiting there to see her off. As soon as she had gone through the departure gate they turned on me like a pack of dogs, demanding that I go back to the Embassy with them as His Excellency the Ambassador was furious. I wasn't sure I wanted to see him and grumbled to Elamu about the unnecessary delay this would cause as I climbed back into the Land Rover. Halfway back from the airport, as we came into a rundown part of city's sprawling suburbs, my vehicle – as if it had a mind of its own – suddenly turned off the main road and drove down a series of narrow lanes through a market area. Two of the embassy cars tried to follow, but it didn't take long to lose them. Half an hour later, Elamu and I were on the road northward, headed back to the desert. As far as I was concerned, all the talking had been done and, if either the development attaché or the Ambassador really wanted to see me, they could come to the desert. They knew where to find me, more or less.

Three weeks later a message arrived at Fred's bar telling me that a new engineer had been appointed. His name was Mike. The message gave a date and flight number in about two weeks time.

10 ~ The seed of an idea

I SPENT MOST OF the intervening time extending my language skills and talking to the Afar about the project. I encouraged them to come to the work site and see what was planned. The model was used countless times to demonstrate how the system worked and I got those who had made the handles to explain how to use the tools.

A small stockpile of flour and powdered milk arrived in Weranzo five days after my visitor's departure but the lorry driver was unwilling to leave the main road and deliver it to my camp. After a fruitless hour spent arguing, I eventually made him unload it all himself and build a pile behind Fred's bar. Mohamed, Elamu and I then loaded and transferred twenty sacks at a time up to the camp in the Land Rover.

A message was sent back with the lorry driver saying that we would require a similar load each week from now on and that it must be delivered to the camp; off-loading at Weranzo village was not acceptable. This rate of supply was more than the food-for-work programme called for but I intended to use the excess to give subsistence food to other starving people in the area since the

The morning queue for food.

main relief effort had still done nothing for them. The additional food they received for work would give them a bonus so they could regain some of the condition they had lost through the drought. It was unrealistic to expect hard work from anyone in the state they were in now; they needed food.

Repercussions were bound to follow, but I'd face them when they occurred.

Within days the Afar encampment near my camp grew until more than fifty *a'aris* were clustered nearby. Each morning, soon after sunrise, I doled out food, and then we went to work. A few of the women began collecting stones and piling them on the river bed upstream of where our weir would be. A few men carried on making handles for shovels and hoes. Work was slow at first, with only ten women and fourteen men doing anything. A lot of other men stood around and watched, but at least a few had got involved and were doing an acceptable job.

When other men realised that those who worked got more food, more began to join in, but our numbers were still very low in proportion to the crowd of people camped nearby.

USING WATER FROM the well, I started a small vegetable garden, growing lettuces, onions and tomatoes. The soil was remarkably fertile and, provided I kept their roots wet, things grew at an astonishing speed. In five weeks I had tomatoes ripening and the Afar looked on enviously as Mohamed, Elamu and I sat eating them.

One day Farasabba Mohamed sidled over and asked if he could have a tomato. I gave him one, asking why he and his friends didn't grow them.

"We don't know how," he replied.

"I didn't know how until I learned," I said. "You could learn, but it needs regular work."

He bit into the tomato and savoured the taste. "Will you show me?" he asked after a pause.

Gotcha!

That was just the opening I was looking for. He would need nurturing, but at least he had opened the door. Together we walked over to the little garden. I raked over a line where nothing was planted and poured water over it. Then I brought out a small packet of seeds, sprinkled some on my hand and showed them to him. I demonstrated how to put them individually into a thumb hole in the damp ground, covering them lightly with more soil and making sure to put them all in a straight line. I poured a few seeds into his palm and encouraged him to have a go. It was easy enough to get the line straight with a couple of small sticks and a piece of string but his fingers were unaccustomed to handling the small seeds and the task took him some time.

"Now you wait," I explained when the line was planted and we had covered it over. "You must keep the soil damp at all times and in a few days there will be small green shoots. I brought a length of shade netting and propped this on sticks over his line, explaining that it would reduce the heat from the sun and slow down the drying of the soil.

For the next few days we watched.

I think Farasabba was ready to give up long before the first small shoots finally appeared, but when I called him over and pointed them out, he got quite excited. He had watered the line four times a day but, not seeing any result, he was beginning to think he had done something wrong. It was strange to see his impatience growing; the Afar are normally remarkably patient people. But his enthusiasm came back tenfold once he saw his seeds growing. He remembered the taste of the tomato I had given him and he wanted tomatoes of his own, now. These minuscule green shoots were going to give him tomatoes in a few weeks. He licked his lips in anticipation and I quietly shared his excitement.

Before the day was out at least fifteen other Afar men had sauntered over to look at Farasabba's green shoots. They could see my plants, growing well and producing tomatoes, but these minute sprouts belonged to one of their own people and thus assumed an almost mystical significance. By the time the plants were six inches high, three other men had asked for help to grow tomatoes.

I was running out of tomato seeds so I got them planting spinach instead. The difference didn't matter; the people were just as excited and their enthusiasm was becoming infectious. I looked forward to the day when one of the women might ask to try, but that, as it turned out, never happened in my time there. This was still new and exciting and therefore men's work. It wouldn't be until they considered it mundane and tedious that the women would be allowed to try. Just like in the rest of Africa, the women

Dodha tribe dagnyas or elders: from left, Ali Manana, the
makaban Doga Detolali, Yusi Digana, Saoumi Amaü and
Farasabba Mohamed.

were second-class citizens who bore the burden of work, while the
men had all the fun and did the 'important' things.

A week after harvesting my first tomato, I went to Weranzo
village to talk to the *makaban*. I was surprised that Doga Detolali
had not been near me or the worksite since we had last spoken as
I felt sure he would be interested in what was going on. It turned
out that he was away, having gone off with two of his sons to take
his herds to distant grazing some days walk to the north-east. I left
word that I would like to talk to him and, after a quick
refreshment stop at Fred's bar, went back to camp.

That afternoon was spent treating a number of minor injuries
and stuffing medicine into a small girl with rampant dysentery
who was getting thinner by the day. Mohamed and I spent a lot of
time explaining to the women the importance of using boiled
water when making up milk from the dried powder I was giving

them. But it was slow work and, like everything else with the Afar, everyone wanted to have his or her say about the matter. One of the problems that emerged from this discussion was that almost none of the women had a decent cooking pot or kettle in which to boil their water, but they were all too embarrassed to say so. Once we discovered this, I put cooking pots on my shopping list.

11 ~ Negotiations

DOGA DETOLALI TURNED UP about three days after my visit to Weranzo. He had heard all about what was going on, which I found encouraging, and had finally come to see it himself. He didn't really need me to give him the guided tour; Farasabba and two others who had planted crops were there watering their vegetable patches and they told him all about it. The first flowers on their plants had opened two days before and it would not be long before the first tomato appeared. It was rewarding to see their enthusiasm. Despite all being grown men, they were like a bunch of school children around a playground gardening plot.

Back at my camp, we sat down to talk over sticky coffee. Most of the Afar preferred tea but I had noticed one or two of them had a distinct liking for this syrupy black brew. It looked like liquid road tar and its taste was about as appealing, but if it kept them here talking, I was happy to provide it. Dispensing generous cups of tea or coffee was proving to be a useful way of spending some of my over-generous per diem allowance.

It didn't take long for the *makaban* to understand that we were nearly ready to start work on the irrigation scheme. A few more essential supplies were due to be delivered in the next ten days and there was another engineer coming to work with me. It was time to talk to the people, to let them all know formally what we were doing and to ask them to work on it. I knew there would still be things to discuss and his help was going to be essential for that to be successful. I asked him to call a meeting and get as many people as possible there so that we could do the talking and start getting on with the work. It was already March. Time was passing and there was a lot of digging and construction to get done before the rains hit the mountains in July or August.

Doga told me the Dodha tribe had four clans, all of which would need to be involved. To complicate matters, the land where the weir was to be situated was in one clan's traditional territory while the field area lay in another's. The other two clans had territory further away but they were still part of the tribe and therefore entitled to participate and benefit from a communal project like this. Looking at the vast open expanse of almost featureless flat land, I wondered how they knew where the boundaries were, but it was clear that they did and that clan territory was fiercely protected, even when both clans belonged to the same tribe. Disagreements and infringements didn't often lead to fighting, but they could result in loud and long-winded arguments which were eventually settled by a minor exchange of livestock.

Word arrived that the next food lorry had dumped its load at Weranzo, so I took Doga back there, along with half a dozen others who fancied a ride in the Land Rover. Except for two who offered token assistance, they watched me load the back of the vehicle and then clung to the outside with youthful enthusiasm as we drove slowly back to camp. It took five more trips to move all the sacks but after the second load, two more of the Afar men offered to help load. For their work they each earned a two-kilo bag of milk powder which I gave them when the last sack was unloaded. They were pleased with their windfall.

While we were loading the milk, I asked Mohamed to wander around the village and tell everyone that we wanted to talk to them tomorrow about the irrigation and there would be tea and food for those who came to talk. I was far from certain that many would turn up but drove back to camp feeling we had made a bit of progress.

The grove of tamarisk trees was quite extensive and my camp occupied only a small area at one end. At the other end there was a natural clearing surrounded by the feathery branches of five sprawling trees which gave at least partial shade for much of the day. In the morning, I set up a hearth in one corner of this clearing and started a fire under a five-gallon pot of water. When this came to the boil I tipped in a whole packet of loose tea and a few minutes later added four pounds of sugar. Elamu took over, raking out most of the fire but keeping enough embers burning so the tea would stay hot. He dispensed tea to every person who turned up.

Before anyone arrived, we made a large batch of chapattis which Elamu and Mohamed handed out with the tea. This kept the crowd interested while we waited for the *makaban* and his elders. By ten o'clock, when Doga Detolali and the other elders turned up, about eighty people had assembled. This was a much bigger group than we had spoken to before and looked promising.

To get things going, I asked Doga if he would tell the people what he understood from our previous talks. He launched into a long and complicated discourse and Mohamed whispered in my ear to explain what he was saying. It sounded to me as if he was making it more complicated than necessary, but I didn't want to dampen this obvious enthusiasm. After about fifteen minutes, Farasabba told everyone about his tomatoes. Everyone had heard it before, of course, and most of them had been to have a look for themselves, but it made good telling and I was all in favour of these chaps encouraging and convincing their own people to become involved. It made my job that much easier and people were more likely to support the scheme if the explanation came from one of their own rather than from an outsider.

Two hours into the talking, Elamu was flagging. Making that many chapattis and doling out tea was tiring work and with the added heat from the fire, it was becoming too much. I suggested he go back to the camp, take a long drink of water and rest for a while.

Realising what was happening, Farasabba called two of the women who were sitting in a group beyond the assembled men, and told them to take over making chapattis. He had been quick to see the opportunities for free food and didn't want it to stop just because the man making it was getting too hot. In his own quiet way, this man was a natural leader who could be very helpful later on in making this project work, or at least in getting the construction done. Whether it would work or not depended on a lot of other factors, not least among them the question of rain in the mountains actually coming down the right channel and reaching our weir.

This thought provoked another series of ideas and I suddenly realised that flow reaching our weir was a question that had received little attention during the survey and planning phases. We had ridden along on the wave of urgency and completely missed what could be a vital point. It was essential that at least a little time should be spent checking before we began building anything.

The scheme would look pretty daft and not help anyone if we built the system and then the water all went somewhere else.

Later, when the talking paused, I asked Farasabba about this. Since I was due to go up the Addis Ababa the following week to collect Mike, it made sense to go a few days early and have a little extra time to talk with other government departments and see if there was some way of checking this out.

We talked with the Dodha for two days and then called a halt. I told them that I had to go and collect the new engineer who was coming to help with the work and we would continue talking when I came back with him. Meanwhile Mohamed would remain in my camp and give out food every day for any work that was done. Everyone seemed satisfied with this.

The next morning Elamu and I left early and headed for the mountains. The quickest way to check whether any water was likely to come down the channel we had chosen was to fly over the area, follow the channel upstream and have a look. If any diversionary work was needed to make sure that flow went in the right direction, it would have to be organised with the local clans. Inevitably that would involve protracted negotiations and we would have to make sure there was some way the clans involved benefited, not just by being fed for the work they did, but when the whole scheme was completed and produced any crop. I could see this getting very complicated and looked forward to having another man around off whom I could bounce ideas.

Organising a flight over the desert was much easier than I expected. We visited the airfield at Kombolcha, which was on our route to the capital anyway, and there found the ideal planes: five small Saab MF19 aircraft owned by Count Carl Gustav von Rosen. The Swedish entrepreneur had based his relief team there and was happy for one of his pilots to fly me over the area. I left Elamu snoozing at the airport office and went flying.

A trip that had taken us nearly four hours by road took only forty minutes in the nippy little Saab. We flew out over the desert at nine thousand feet in the hope of staying cool and followed the main road until we reached Weranzo. From there it was only a few minutes until we were circling over the worksite from where we followed the channel upstream. I took a few photographs and drew sketches of the channel layout, noting the points at which it might be inclined to change direction and trying to fix their exact positions so that they could later be inspected on the ground.

This would have been simple with a GPS gadget, but such things hadn't been invented then, so fixing the position was a laborious task. It involved checking several intersecting compass headings and recording these on a sketch of the ground, noting any nearby features that might also be visible from ground level.

We noted four possible diversion points before we started running low on fuel and headed back to Kombolcha. The pilot offered to make another flight the next day but by now I was tight for time and had to decline. He offered to go back without me now that he understood what I had been looking for, and drop me a message at my camp if he found anything. He would try and get permission from the Count. We parted with a handshake and I climbed back into the Land Rover which Elamu drove until we stopped for the night in Debre Berhan.

THE FLIGHT BRINGING Mike was on time the following morning and we only just reached the airport as the first passengers were coming out of the arrivals hall. I had no idea what he looked like and had to hope I could pick him out of the crowd. Fortunately he guessed that the only European waiting, a ragged, blond-haired man with a beard, might be me and came striding over. He was a man of about my own age, similarly bearded and I liked him immediately.

Courtesy demanded that I take Mike to the LMB offices and introduce him and as a result we managed to waste the rest of the day there. Our visit was not entirely unproductive as we learned that a new District Governor had been appointed for Bati. We also managed to get our hands on a second Land Rover.

Someone in the LMB office suggested that we might find it useful to have a camp manager cum cook with us in the desert, and after some discussion, we had the names of several men who would call on us at our hotel later. If one was suitable, he could come to the desert with us immediately. It sounded a bit like the LMB managers were trying to encumber us with staff of their choosing. We wondered what their purpose was in doing so but got no clear explanation. At the same time, having someone else around who could do the cooking sounded good to us, so we agreed to meet the men and finally escaped from the offices at about six-thirty.

Half an hour later, the first of the hopefuls arrived. He spoke not a word of English and there was some doubt whether he could cook anything, so we told him the office would be in touch and sent him on his way. Two more men followed, both eminently unsuitable and looking disenchanted with the whole idea when they heard that they would be working in the Danakil. As the last one left, the hotel steward, who had overheard some of our discussions, suggested he knew a man we might like to meet. We told him what the job was and said that if, knowing all that, his man was interested, we would be pleased to talk to him. The steward asked if we would mind talking to him somewhere else as the man was apprehensive about coming into the hotel.

At the steward's suggestion, we went to a small café in the square and bought a flask of Tej and some coffee. About twenty minutes later, the steward arrived with an older man whom he introduced as Tadese Waldewariat. We asked them both to join us but the steward said he had to go back to the hotel. The other man sat down and accepted coffee.

Tadese turned out to be a most intriguing man. He said he wasn't much good at cooking European food because it was many years since he had been required to do this. But he understood Ethiopian cuisine and he was willing to learn. Now in his late sixties, he had begun his working life as a muleteer in the army of Haile Selassie, when he was taking the Empire back from the Italians, and had done all sorts of things since then, including being a cook for a number of years. Although he could read and write in both Coptic script and English, he claimed not to be well educated, but it soon became apparent that he was a man stuffed with useful knowledge and experience. It didn't take long to realise that his membership of our team could be a great asset. In addition, unlike most of the mountain people, he was not in the least afraid of going to the Danakil and living among the Afar. By the time we had finished the coffee, we had hired him and asked him to be at our hotel by seven the next morning ready to go. Because of the way we arranged it, Tadese was employed by Mike and me, not by the LMB, which pleased him and us but caused mild apoplexy among the Ethiopian officials who thought they should be in charge of our staff and wanted to control everything. Later, this proved to be a very good decision; Tadese was worth every dollar we paid him.

Tadese was worth every dollar we paid him.

"Just one thing," I asked Tadese before he left us that evening, "how do you know the hotel steward?"

With a note of pride he replied, "He is my second son."

AT SEVEN THE NEXT MORNING when we were about to set out with two Land Rovers, a load more camping kit and tools and a supply of dried food including rice and pasta which we hoped might make our diet a little varied, trouble turned up in the form of Ato Abaye. He was the manager responsible for the food-for-work programmes the LMB currently had running. Three of these were located in the south-west of the country, in the Omo River valley, and another one was in Wollo, near Bati. He informed us that with immediate effect our mission had been included in his remit. He therefore needed to have a conference with us to find out what we were doing and to gather details. This seemed unnecessary but we decided we'd better humour him, so we went to his office and spent an hour telling him about the project. As we were about to leave, he announced that he had another project which we were required to fulfil and he would now brief us on that. We looked at one another with some surprise and waited to see what this was about.

It turned out that Ato Abaye had agreed with persons unknown in London that we would go into the mountains not far from Addis Ababa and spend a few days restoring a water catchment reservoir. He had approached HMG who had given him a letter instructing us to comply with his wishes. It was signed by the development attaché at the Embassy and dated two weeks previously. I wondered why the Embassy hadn't informed me of this before and concluded this was someone being stuffy because I hadn't warned them about the director's visit. Pettiness takes many forms but this amounted to interference with the mission. I was about to say the development attaché could go to hell when I looked a little more closely at the letter. At the bottom it also bore another set of initials which I recognised as belonging to one of the grey man's staff. This changed everything.

I went into another office and rang the contact at the Embassy. We talked for a long time and finally I could see some value in what was proposed. Without telling Mike why I had changed my mind, I told Ato Abaye we would give him four days.

So, for the next four days we worked on building a new water tank at the transmitter station for Radio Voice of the Gospel. The original plan had been to resurrect an existing tank, but this was in such a derelict state it was not worth the work. There was plenty of open space and a digger was available to carve a new pit, forty-five feet square and ten feet deep. Into this we put a double layer of thick polythene and from the base upwards we covered it with slim polythene sausages filled with a dry cement and sand mixture. The back of these sausages was punctured with a line of small holes made by laying each one on a plank studded with nails moments before it was placed in position. Once the tank was full, water would seep into the sausages and the cement would set, leaving a solid lining in the tank when the polythene tubing eventually degraded in the sunlight.

Early on the fourth morning, as soon as the lining was complete, we put enough water into the tank to check it was watertight. Leaving the radio station staff to work out how to cover the new reservoir and stop their water evaporating, we headed for Bati before Ato Abaye could think of anything else to distract us.

I had discovered that he had never been in favour of our project. He thought that the Afar were a waste of time; an inferior

Starting to line the new tank with 'sausages'.

people who should be left alone to sort out their own problems. He was clearly afraid of them and only ever came to the desert once during the time we worked there. Even then he couldn't wait to get away again. This diversion was the first time he actively interfered, but unfortunately it wasn't to be the last.

WE STOPPED BRIEFLY at Debre Berhan for lunch. The café owner was pleased to see us and produced an excellent meal. Mike tucked in as if he had been eating *injera* for years. After lunch we carried on and drove into the hotel yard in Bati long after dark.

There was a message waiting at the hotel saying that the District Governor was back at his office and wanted to see me as soon as possible. After what we had heard in Addis Ababa, I assumed he wanted to have one last go at telling me off before handing over to the new man.

There was also a somewhat terse message from Ato Abaye saying that we should not have left without seeing him. There were issues which needed to be resolved before we went down to the desert and he instructed us to wait until either he or Ato Hapteab, the local LMB representative, contacted us. I was already beginning to be distrustful of Abaye's motives and this did nothing to dispel my doubts. We decided that if Hapteab had not turned up by the time we were ready to go in the morning, we would just go anyway. If he really wanted to talk to us, he could come to Weranzo. This would tell us whether the matter was important.

12 ~ New governor, new start

ALTHOUGH THERE WAS no reason why Mike should become embroiled in my spat with the District Governor, he decided to come when I went to his office the next morning. Perhaps having him there might take some steam out of the governor's pique. It was fortuitous that he did come because Ato Gabre Yuhannou, the man with whom I had crossed swords, had already left. The man wanting to see us was his replacement, Bimbashi Tefera Waldemariam, who had arrived only two days before.

Tefera was a robust, friendly man, immediately interested in what we were doing in the desert and dismayed to hear that aid was not already reaching the Afar. He promised not only to come and see for himself very soon, but to unblock the channels and make sure things that had been promised were delivered. He was a positive, can-do sort of man who was like a breath of fresh air. Although I was predisposed to be suspicious of promises made by officials, somehow I found myself believing this one. There was something different about this man we couldn't help liking. We felt upbeat as we drove down to the desert that afternoon.

While we had been at the governor's office, Tadese had been to the market in Bati and stocked up on fresh fruit and veg. He appeared to have bought far too much and I could see us either giving most of it away before it shrivelled up, or having to eat so much before it went off that we burst. I wondered how he thought we were going to keep all that fresh produce with no refrigerator, but I needn't have worried; he knew exactly what he was doing.

After a corned beef hash supper, Tadese busied himself with some unspecified task under the tree beside his tent while Mike and I sat down with the system plans to discuss how we would go about setting out and getting work started. He would set out the weir first and work out how much of the bank needed to be excavated to make the takeoff channel and the head works for the main channel. As soon as that was done we could start getting stones positioned in the river bed next to where they would be required for building the weir.

By the time we went to bed, Tadese had constructed himself a

Tadese and his camp kitchen.

bush refrigerator out of hessian sacking, a can full of water and a lot of string and sticks. It looked ridiculous but, as we discovered over the next few days, it worked remarkably well.

The weir was to be a gabion structure some sixty-five feet across, six feet wide and rising about five feet out of the river bed. Gabions, large wire baskets filled with carefully packed stones and wired together, make an ideal construction medium for this type of weir. They allow some water to pass over, or even through the structure, while holding up most of it for diversion down a channel. In our weir we were going to include a neoprene membrane to let less of the flow pass though the structure in the hope of retaining a pond above the weir after the flow had ceased. Barriers of this sort are strong and flexible enough to withstand the forces imposed by a sudden rush of water such as we hoped to catch here.

A supply of materials had already been organised and the first gabions were due to arrive the next week. Some would also be used at other points in the system to add strength where channels changed direction, but these structures had yet to be designed.

After an early breakfast, I asked Tadese to come and help with the morning food distribution before we began work on the site. I was hoping that once he got used to it, he would be willing to take over some of this work. It would save us a lot of time and Tadese seemed like the sort of man who would do it fairly and without fuss. He soon got the idea, but told me later he didn't like the smell of rancid butter these people carried with them. I assured him he would cease to notice it after a few days, but he wrinkled his nose all the same and said he didn't think that was possible, one could never get used to that smell. It was the only time he ever grumbled or said anything negative about the Afar.

Mike was adept with his theodolite and level. In three hours, there were white lines drawn across the river bed and dozens of pegs marking out the head works. There were also batter boards showing the slopes we needed to cut where the channel began. It wasn't long before we were ready to start digging. Now all that was needed was to get the Afar's agreement.

AS IF SENSING that things had reached a critical point, that was when the Afar decided it was time to talk again. People had been interested in what we were doing while we were setting out and it had been relatively easy to explain, once more with the aid of the model, what this had all been about. We found that one man had pulled out a number of our pegs and brought them with him to ask what they were for and why we had banged them into the ground. While this was frustrating, it was also quite amusing and it took Mike and Mohamed half an hour to explain to the man why the pegs had been put where they were and why they should

Pegging out: Mike took to numbering the pegs.

Inspecting the Weranzo weir site.

be left there. They had no sooner finished and replaced the pegs when someone else brought a peg from the far side of the weir and asked if this one had the same purpose. In the end they had to walk round and describe the meaning of every one of the fifty or so pegs installed that morning and ask everyone to make sure they remained where they were. Just as a precaution the pegs were numbered from then on to make it easier to replace them in the correct position if any more should be brought in for discussion.

After the pegs, they wanted to talk about other things, including who worked where, how much food they would get for their efforts and how long we would work each day. They also said they needed medicine as many of their people were too sick to work and it was not fair on the sick if they couldn't earn food. All these were good points which had hardly been touched on in previous discussions.

In the end we agreed to work gangs that suited their family and clan affiliations. We told them how much food they would receive and, while some wanted to argue about this, it was presented as a take it or leave it deal, which truncated the talking considerably. It was a pity we weren't in a position to use that ploy more often, but at least it worked on that occasion.

We had discovered earlier that the people in the nearby encampment needed decent cooking pots and other things, but we hoped to resolve this soon. Actually I was pinning my hopes on the new District Governor. When we met him in Bati, I had mentioned that such items were sorely needed and hoped he would be able to include some in his aid package. If he kept his word about making sure we got aid in the desert, it would make a lot of things easier.

It was mid-afternoon before the discussion broke up and the Afar returned to their encampment. There were about two hundred people there by now. This was still far too few to accomplish the work we were undertaking but for the moment it was all we could cope with. Still, it didn't stop me worrying about how we were going to recruit more workers. I decided to have another talk with the *makaban* the next time I went to Weranzo.

13 ~ More relief, more work

FIVE DAYS LATER, just after we had stopped work at one o'clock to rest through the hottest part of the day, I got news that two aid lorries would be coming down the main road later that day. We took both Land Rovers and headed for Fred's bar in the hope that, if the story was true, we could intercept them.

An hour later the first lorry arrived, a Bedford three-tonner in green military colours with a soldier at the wheel. Sitting in the passenger seat with a big grin on his face was our new District Governor. He had brought a mixed load of things the Afar needed and he wanted to deliver them himself to make sure they were given out fairly and not hoarded like the maize pyramid still standing beside the police post.

He walked over to look at this and insisted that the cover was removed. To the horror of the watching policemen who had been guarding them, he ripped open several sacks with a knife and let the grain spill out onto the ground. Picking up a handful, he inspected it and offered it to the senior policeman, asking him how he should prepare it for eating. The policeman looked sheepish and said he didn't know. Clearly angry, Tefera said he

The District Governor's aid arrives in Weranzo village.

didn't know either as the grain was now shrivelled and useless. If it had been distributed when it arrived it might have had some value. As it was, the whole lot was wasted. He was very cross about the waste and became even more so when the policeman said that he had only been following the orders he had been given.

Tefera set the two policemen to unloading the truck he had arrived in. Another lorry arrived as they were finishing and he told them to unload this as well. Meanwhile he wanted to speak to the *balabat* and the *makaban*. When Doga Detolali arrived, Tefera introduced himself and asked who among his people most needed the goods he had brought. There was food and milk powder, a few pots and pans, blankets, lengths of cloth, dozens of tin and plastic cups and even a few metal bowls. In a few minutes a crowd had gathered and the supplies were distributed.

Once everything had been given away, Tefera asked to be taken to our worksite. He wanted to see what we were actually doing. We left the two lorries at Fred's bar and, together with one or two of the Afar elders, headed into the desert in our Land Rovers. On the site, Mike explained the engineering and I told him about the workforce and how we were dealing with the people. We took this opportunity to raise the question of medical assistance, walking him round some of the *a'aris* where we knew there were sick people. It was Tefera's first exposure to the Afar and it had a profound effect on him. When we took him back to the village, I handed him a shopping list of other things these people desperately needed.

He was very positive, thanking us for our efforts and apologising that his office had previously taken no interest in our work. That, he assured us, would definitely change now that he was in charge. He took my list and said he would see what was available, inviting us to call on him next time we came to Bati, at whatever time of day or night we arrived.

Taking the two policemen and all their kit with him in the back of his truck, Tefera went back to Bati, saying he would be back in a few days. We would be getting new policemen to occupy the police post, he added; somebody who would be useful, not two laggards dumped there as a punishment which they clearly deserved. He didn't say what was going to happen to the two men he was taking away, but I suspected it would not be entirely pleasant. If they were lucky he would just sack them and send them back to their own villages.

Before we left the village to go back to camp, Doga Detolali approached us and said, "You kept your promise and brought help. That was good. The people will remember that."

I was pleased with that bit of recognition and hoped it would smooth our future relations with the Afar.

The following morning, ten new men volunteered for work.

14 ~ A taste of the truth

WE STARTED DIGGING the following day, but didn't move a lot of earth because work started very slowly and the Afar men proved to be far less competent at using the tools than we had hoped. It was necessary to show each man individually how to hold a shovel or a hoe and then watch what he did with it until he got the right idea. We kept records of who used which tools so that they could be given the same one each day.

Once the tools had been handed out, I gathered groups of five men, stood them in a line and went along showing each man where to put his hands and how to grip the handle. When they all had the correct grip, I stood out in front of the line and showed them all how to dig into the ground and lift out a clod of soil.

Digging with a spade is simple if it's something you have done all your life, but it was completely alien to these men. We cheered and applauded when one of them got it right and encouraged those who didn't until gradually they all got the idea. Once one group was started I moved on to another, keeping an eye on the first lot to make sure they kept digging and kept trying to do it right, occasionally going back to encourage them or to move them

Gradually the workers mastered the unfamiliar tools.

along so that they didn't dig too deep in the same spot. For that first day, my records show we moved only about three cubic metres of earth. Much of this was moved by Mike and me showing the Afar how to dig, but it was a start.

Work stopped at one o'clock and each man received the food ration he had earned that day. The women who had been collecting stones along the river bed were also paid with food, but there were only a few of them and their rations didn't take long to distribute. Each adult received the same amount, regardless of gender and from that day onwards, the food given to those who didn't work was only half what the workers earned. This was soon understood by the Afar. Day by day the workforce grew, only by ones and twos at first, but gradually more people were willing to try.

At the end of that first week, Tefera came again, with two more lorries loaded with milk powder and flour together with lots of other useful items from my list. He reached Weranzo at the same time as the first truck load of gabions we had been expecting. The driver of this vehicle was all for dumping his load in the village and returning as fast as he could to his depot in Dessie, but Tefera intervened and told him that if he didn't deliver them to the worksite he would be arrested and his truck would be impounded. The man reluctantly agreed and followed Tefera's lorry across the desert. The governor's second wagon followed behind to prevent the reluctant truck driver turning back.

That Thursday we stopped work early and the Afar who had enlisted to work helped unload the three trucks. I told them this task was also counted as work and they would get their food ration for it as usual. It was all that was needed to get an enthusiastic gang off-loading everything and the reluctant truck driver racing back along the tracks he had made coming, to get on the road and back to the mountains as fast as possible. It was only after the driver had left that we realised he had delivered only about half the number of gabions listed on the manifest. In addition, some were of a size we had not ordered and did not want.

I leapt into the Land Rover and set off in pursuit, taking a direct route across the desert to intersect the road just east of the village and hoping to get ahead of the truck which had followed the more circuitous route it had taken coming in. With his vehicle empty, the driver had made better time than I realised and he had already reached the road and gone past the point where I joined it. When I caught up with him at Eliwoha where, fortunately, he stopped to talk to a friend at the police post, he told me he had brought everything that was loaded and didn't know one gabion from another so wouldn't have been able to check anyway. He had brought the load that Ato Abaye had signed out of the store.

Ato Abaye again; the mention of his name immediately rang alarm bells. I looked at the manifest again. It was made out in his handwriting and several items had been crossed off completely. Clearly, this was nothing short of deliberate interference with something he neither understood nor had any authority over. I was furious. All these goods were being paid for by HMG; they were none of his business. The only responsibility LMB staff had was to provide transport and that was part of a contractual agreement.

I asked the driver when he was due to bring the next load but he said there was nothing else to bring.

"What about the food delivery tomorrow?"

"There is none on the schedule."

I thanked him for his help and let him go on his way. I would be going to Dessie in a few days for the next relief committee meeting and could check in the LMB stores myself.

AS I WAS ABOUT TO leave Eliwoha, one of the Afar men hanging around the village asked me if I could give him some medicine for his wife. Enquiring what was wrong with her, I discovered that she was in great pain. A huge sore on her arm was eating the flesh away. I asked the man to show me.

The Afar are very protective of their women and don't usually allow anyone to talk to them either directly or alone, so it didn't

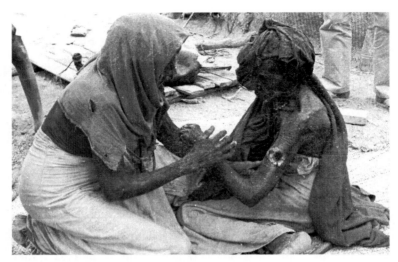

The woman had an open wound with flesh eaten to the bone.

surprise me that he first gathered several other women to sit with his wife and then got their husbands to stand around the outside of her hut. When I was eventually led in, it was to see the woman sitting facing away from me with just her scrawny arm exposed.

It was wrapped in a grubby rag, which was tied roughly round the upper arm to cover the wound. Despite the smoky smell of the *a'ari* and the cheesy aroma of the husband's hair, the stench of rotting flesh was strong from fifteen feet away. I wondered what I was going to see when the cloth was removed but was not prepared for what I found.

The wound was spectacular. The hole in the woman's arm was at least two inches across; her flesh was raw down to the bone, red, angry and pus laden. I asked the man what had happened: had his wife been bitten, or gashed by a spike of wood? He said nothing like that had happened. The hole had just grown. It started some weeks after a government health team had come and vaccinated some of the women.

"What did they vaccinate for?" I asked, being at the time in complete ignorance of the visit made by the smallpox team.

The man didn't know but one of the others told me they had left a lot of little bottles and other things. These were still lying where the men had worked. He led me through the cluster of huts and showed me the scatter of empty vaccine ampoules. I collected them all, together with half a dozen small metal lancets, and put them in a plastic bag from my first aid kit. From the labels it was clear they had contained smallpox vaccine, made by an eastern European manufacturer. The expiry date had passed five years previously.

"When was this done?" I asked.

"Only three and a half moons ago," the man replied. That made it about three weeks before I first came to the desert. I felt sick and angry.

Using dressings and disinfectant from the first aid kit, I cleaned the woman's arm as well as I could, applied a clean dressing and promised to come back in a few days and do it again. It was only as I was packing up that anyone said there were other women with equally big sores which also needed attention. In all there were thirty-four of them. Some of the younger women had little more than small open scars, but many others, particularly the older women, had huge bone-deep craters. Something had gone horribly wrong here.

They said their arms had itched badly and this had made them scratch the vaccination scabs. To make matters worse, some of the women had collected torch batteries, thrown from their cabs by passing lorry drivers, and used the caustic gel they contained to cover the wound in an attempt to stop the incessant itching. One or two had even melted lumps of tar and applied this to their wounds as if to cauterise them.

None of the men had any wound since none of them had allowed the health team to vaccinate them. They were quick to link the events and identify the vaccination as the root cause. This did not bode well for any future public health initiative in the area. They would never trust a government health team again.

With the limited resources available in the first aid kit, I did the best I could. When I came back in a few days, I would have more supplies to help those I couldn't help now. I would also ask the doctors at the relief camps in Bati for their help. My camera was in the car and for once it had a film in it, so I took a few photographs as evidence along with the bag of empty ampoules.

My anger at Ato Abaye's interference was temporarily forgotten as I drove away, wondering if there were women with similar injuries all along the road the health team had travelled. As I passed back through Weranzo, I called on Doga Detolali to ask if any of the Dodha women had ulcerated arms. He had not heard of any but a few days later some women appeared in the camp with similar sores. They too had been vaccinated and, after hearing about my visit to Eliwoha, had decided to seek my help. The fact that the women were prepared to come forward and ask for help was a milestone in the establishment of trust.

My return to camp was greeted with the news that a young girl had been bitten by a snake in the bush a few miles away and had died as a result. Writing in the project diary later, I noticed the date on the blank page. It was my birthday.

THREE DAYS LATER I went to Dessie to attend the relief committee meeting. This time the Governor General decided to attend in person instead of sending one of his minions. Security was an issue I wanted to raise. We had been getting regular reports that the Issa had again crossed the frontier from Somalia and were raiding the southern Afar tribes for livestock. In addition, with my recent discovery of the damage done by the smallpox vaccinations and the lack of any relief until that delivered by the new District Governor just the previous week, I had a few crows to pluck. This was my opportunity.

When the Enderassie began to pontificate about how efficient his staff had been at coordinating the international relief effort, I saw that most of the representatives of the foreign agencies looked scandalised. Nevertheless they sat there mute and let him ramble on for a full ten minutes. At no point did he mention the desert people or their needs; for all he appeared to care, they might not have existed. As he began his closing remarks I stood up, interrupted and asked what he was doing for the Afar.

His reply told it all. "There is no problem in the desert and no need for relief," he said. "We are fully occupied with the situation in the mountains and the camps around Bati."

That was too much for me. With the rashness of youth, I let him have a full broadside salvo. I had managed to get the photographs taken in Eliwoha a few days earlier developed the previous night. Now I dropped glossy eight-by-ten-inch pictures on the table as I recounted what his health team had done. I tossed half the empty ampoules in a scatter across the table for emphasis. I went on and told everyone about the pyramids of grain being guarded by policemen until they shrivelled in the sun, while the pigeons and the rats got fatter and the people got thinner. I told them about the disruption caused by raiding tribesmen from across the border and how my repeated requests for the authorities in general, and the Enderassie's office in particular, to do something to prevent them from coming had been ignored. I

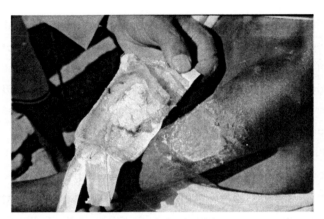

Photographic evidence of the health team's work.

told him about the dysentery and fevers being experienced by the Afar and the total lack of any medical care. Then I told him about the locusts that had been discovered breeding near our worksite, just two days earlier.

The Enderassie sat looking stunned, sour and angry while I spoke. When I stopped he got up and walked out without saying a word. There were a few moments of stupefied silence as I sat down before the room erupted. I guessed there would be repercussions later, but after what I had seen during the last few days, I was beyond caring about that.

Unbeknown to me, there was a British journalist called Christopher Dobson sitting at the back of the room. He was from the *Daily Telegraph* and had been taking shorthand notes of everything said. As the meeting dispersed, he tapped my elbow and asked if he could buy me lunch. He would very much like to hear more and if he could help... well, maybe he could come down to the desert and see for himself?

I was beginning to calm down by then and he seemed a personable sort of chap. He had obviously done his homework on the region and was willing to do more than just listen, so I accepted his invitation to lunch and we talked for over an hour. Afterwards he accompanied me when I went to the LMB store to find out what had happened to the rest of our gabions and the next food delivery. He was very interested to discover there were elements within the Ethiopian hierarchy who were not moving in the same direction when it came to the famine relief and aid programmes.

He also offered some interesting observations on the social unrest that had recently shown its face among younger, educated members of society in this country. Things in Ethiopia were not as serene as appeared on the surface.

This was something that interested me and other people in London. It was something to which I had quietly been paying attention and so it was interesting to get his perspective. The Abyssinian Empire had rolled along for centuries as a feudal society with its provinces ruled by warlord princes – the Rases. Lij Teferi Makonnen, now known as Haile Selassie, had served as regent from 1916 onwards, but finally took the throne as Emperor, King of Kings and Conquering Lion of the Tribe of Juda in 1926, although his coronation was not until 1930.

Abyssinia, as it was then known, was a backward place in those days, not much advanced from the sort of society in Britain soon after the Crusades. Haile Selassie set about changing that but was smart enough to realise that that you cannot bring people out of the Middle Ages and into the glare of the twentieth century overnight. His efforts were interrupted for a few years after 1934, when his empire was occupied by the Italians, but together with General Orde Wingate, Colonel Daniel Sandford and some other wild young men, he led a counter-revolution which eventually reclaimed his country. Haile Selassie was restored to the throne in 1942. Later he renamed the country Ethiopia.

Haile Selassie restarted his reform and modernisation programmes but again had to move slowly due to instability in several of the northern provinces. This was most notably in Tigray and Eritrea; the latter was demanding independence. Even so, by the 1970s he had brought Ethiopian society forward to the equivalent of the late Victorian era in Britain with small sectors reaching forward into the twentieth century. Addis Ababa had become host to the administrative base of the Organisation of African Unity and the country was at last a recognised player on the world stage.

But it wasn't fast enough for the young educated elite who were beginning to flex their muscles. The Eritrean question, which had been more or less settled for a long time, raised its head again and the people there were once more demanding independence. On top of all this the country was beset by drought and Rases like the Enderassie in Dessie were being particularly prickly about their status. The advances in social reform and democracy Haile Selassie had achieved before had now all but ground to a halt. The emperor was no longer in the full flush of youth. He was reputed to have been born in 1897, but it could have been earlier and fifty-seven years bearing the burden of supreme authority had taken its toll.

LATER THAT DAY, after a few more visits around Dessie, Christopher Dobson accompanied me down to the desert to get a first-hand perspective on the situation there. I took him first to Eliwoha to see the effects of the botched smallpox vaccinations. He saw the pyramids of useless grain which still stood there and at Weranzo, ignored, forgotten and wasted. He came out to the worksite and we showed him what we were doing, explaining how we hoped to catch the runoff from the mountain monsoon and use it to grow crops. By the time I took him back the following day, including a visit to the huge relief camp at Bati on the way, he had seen drought face to face, endured the searing 145-degree desert heat and been witness to the mass of humanity dying as they waited in queues at the relief stations, desperately hanging onto the merest hope of life.

Hardened correspondent though he was, accustomed to seeking out humanity's ugliest faces, Dobson found this profoundly moving and more than once I noticed him wiping his eyes. By the time he left me, I was sure he understood the reason for my outburst at the relief committee. He promised to make use of what he had heard and seen. Two weeks later he did, and wrote two long articles which appeared on successive weeks, about the whole mess that was the drought relief effort in Ethiopia. Large pieces of his text were taken verbatim from the things I had said at that meeting in Dessie and during the time he spent with me.

Before leaving, he asked for my family's phone number and kindly called my father from the arrivals hall at Heathrow to say he had seen me and that I was alive and working hard. Letters home from the desert took a long time to arrive, so my family were glad of the news, having heard almost nothing from me for more than two months. It's easy to forget that only a few decades ago communication was a much more protracted business than it is now.

AFTER DROPPING Dobson in Kombolcha to get a flight back to the capital, I called at the Bati camp again to consult one of the doctors about the health problems in the desert. It was clear nobody here was able to offer us any direct medical aid, but at least he could tell me how to deal with the smallpox wounds. From talking to him, I went to the nearest pharmacy and spent a month's worth of my per diem allowance on medicines and dressings. Even what would be classified as prescription drugs in UK were freely available here and could be bought in large quantities. I was able to buy antibiotic pills by the kilo, along with the other items on the doctor's list, so I came away with three large boxes of dressings, swabs, disinfectant and even needles and sutures, and another two boxes of drugs. We were now equipped to treat wounds, infections, dysentery, worms and numerous other common complaints. It was clear that from now on we were going to have to provide a basic medical service as well as doing the construction work until proper medical service could be arranged. I just hoped we didn't accidentally poison anyone.

15 ~ Crime and punishment

WORK WAS GETTING GOING properly now that relief had begun to arrive and the Afar could see that what we had promised was not just a passing wind. They recognised that when we said we would do something, we did it, so the people began to have faith and to respond – slowly. Apart from that, those who worked were being better fed than anyone had been for a long time and the adult wage was calculated to make sure that the children got enough too. If all the adults in a family worked, they did well, and people began to recover from the deep starvation they had experienced for so long. This brought a steady trickle of new recruits and we saw the numbers on the roll increase daily.

Because the Afar were nominally Muslims, we saved Fridays as rest days. We also started paying for work on a weekly basis to ensure that people stayed around, with small bonuses for those who had worked more weeks. So Friday also became pay day.

Weeks began to roll by and there was real progress to be seen on the worksite. The takeoff from the weir was beginning to take shape where the first gabions had been installed, packed with stones and laced up tight. We had dug a shallow trench across the

Engineering department: Mike prepares drawings.

river bed where the weir itself was to be built so that the bottom layer of gabions could be set into a firm base. The first line of baskets had been laid out, opened and their sides wired together ready for filling.

Work had begun on digging the upper section of the main channel that would carry water from the takeoff down to the fields. It was important that this was dug accurately and so sloping batter boards and markers had been installed along the first two hundred yards of its route to provide reference points. We spent a lot of time teaching the digging gangs how to dig accurately to these reference markers.

It was while the first section of the slope above the channel was being graded that the first sign of trouble appeared. One particular man seemed to have a lot to say for himself but every time I came near enough to hear exactly what he was saying, he stopped talking. I asked Mohamed to have a quiet word with the group and tell them that if they had a complaint, I would be happy to hear it and discuss it with them.

Things seemed to settle down but two days later, a pair of men came and asked how long I intended staying in their desert. I asked why this was an issue and they told me they thought our being here and this work were not good for their people and they wished we would leave now. I asked if they wanted the food supplies to stop, as they surely would if we left. After a few more grumbles they walked off sulkily.

Two days later, as I was walking back to camp from the worksite in the late afternoon, a man I did not know but vaguely recognised, stepped from behind a thorn thicket and threw his spear at me. It pierced my leg. This was the first sign of hostility that we had seen since coming to the Danakil and it came as a complete surprise. The impact of the spear had me staggering backwards, straight into another thorn bush. By the time I had pulled the spear out and looked up, there was no one to be seen.

Tied together, my shoelaces were just long enough to serve as a tourniquet. I wound it tight and hobbled back to camp using the spear as support. Mike and Mohamed and Tadese had already gone to the village so I sat and cleaned the wound myself. The spear had a heavy head but was not sharp. Even so it had penetrated at least two and a half inches into the muscle of my thigh. The wound was extremely painful. I took a morphine pill, packed the hole with antibiotic powder and inserted two stitches to close it. After that I swallowed a strong dose of antibiotics to prevent infection and strapped the leg tightly with an elastic bandage and a thick gauze pad over the wound.

We were due to take Tadese to Bati market in a few days to buy vegetables, so I used that opportunity to see the doctor in the relief camp. In the event, the doctor was reassuring. He said the spear tip had missed all the important bits in my leg and it should heal all right. He put a massive injection of antibiotic into my leg, using a needle that seemed to be as thick as coat hanger wire and told me to keep taking the pills I had already started. Time would tell, but he thought I had been lucky.

I kept the spear.

MEANWHILE, I was somewhat immobilised; I wouldn't be able to drive like this and couldn't walk far. When we started work the morning after I was attacked, there was no sign of the man I thought had thrown the spear. Since I couldn't be sure who had done it, I decided to let the matter drop. Mohamed had spoken to the *dagnyas* and told them this sort of behaviour was not acceptable and everyone would lose their food if the project stopped. I had to hope they would ensure people knew this.

Being unable to walk properly, I took to going to the worksite on a mule. We had brought three riding beasts down from the mountains with the intention of trying to plough with them, but didn't yet have any sort of plough. The mules needed to be ridden regularly to keep them fit.

Riding a mule while my leg was injured, particularly on a traditional Ethiopian saddle, is one of the most uncomfortable experiences I've ever had. The beast has a backbone that sticks through the saddle padding; it feels like sitting on a string of walnuts. As the mule moves, they dig into your backside and within a few hundred yards the pain this causes becomes excruciating. I tried using two pads and even sitting side-saddle, but this made the animal uncontrollable.

In the end, the problem was solved for me. Someone took a

pot shot at me and my mule slumped dead beneath me, tipping me into a thorn bush as it went down.

Once again, I didn't see who it was. Everything happened so suddenly. It was early evening and the light was already fading. With a rifle, the attacker could shoot from a long way away and I wasn't certain which direction the shot had come from. There was nothing I could do for the mule so I pulled the saddle and bridle off, hung them in a thorn bush to collect later and left the dead beast for the hyenas. It was only about five hundred yards back to camp and later that night we could hear the pack snarling and yipping as they feasted. In the morning there was little more than a patch of blood-soaked ground, two hooves and an ear to show where the mule had fallen.

SEVERAL WEEKS AFTER this incident, when I was able to walk normally again, I was aware of a new undercurrent among two groups of men digging the main channel. Once again there was a

Digging the main channel at the angle shown by the batter board in the foreground.

lot of talking that faded to silence every time I approached. When I asked, the men claimed they had only been discussing family news, but their shifty looks and general edginess could not hide their tenseness, and this told another story. One man looked vaguely familiar, but I had not yet learned his name. Although he appeared to be at the centre of the chatter, I didn't have enough evidence to accuse him of anything and thought it might just die out if I left well alone.

It didn't, but the men were working well so I decided to wait.

After a few days, the talk changed to chanting. At first this seemed to be nothing more than a way of getting into a rhythmic pattern of work and I let it go on, but gradually he introduced words that told another story. It was clear to me that the man was encouraging rivalry between two clans and that could rapidly get out of hand. The quality of the work being done by the men he worked among was also slipping.

The custom of the Afar when they want to remonstrate with someone in such a situation is to take the offender by the wrist and lead him a few yards away, but still within range for everyone to hear what is said. Several of the men from other clans had already reacted and I decided something must be done to nip this in the bud before it became a major problem. As I reached out to take the man's wrist he raised his shovel and brought it down flat on top of my head.

Fortunately for me, he was not adept in wielding the shovel and I managed to duck and take most of the blow on my shoulders. Even so, he raised it to try again and others around him decided to join in. Within seconds there was a screaming mob, hacking and thrashing with shovels and hoes, trying to bash my head in. Their milling feet in the soft soil stirred up clouds of dust and it was impossible to see what was going on. I dropped onto hands and knees and crawled out between their legs collecting a few sharp thumps from their flying tools on the way, but managing to evade anything really damaging. I also got both knees encrusted with spiny *tribulus* seeds, but that was by the by.

A minute later I was seated on a rock twenty feet away, picking the spiky little caltrops from my skin. The group continued hacking at nothing. As soon as one of them realised where I was, everything stopped. One by one they dropped their tools, all looking slightly foolish like naughty schoolboys caught scrumping fruit.

After staring at them in silence for a few moments, I told them to go home, work was over for the day. Nobody on this part of the site would be paid for their work today. There would be no work for anybody tomorrow and everybody who normally worked would go hungry as a result. No relief food would be given out either. It was the fault of those who had been fighting that all the people would suffer. We would resume work in two days' time, I said, but only if their *makaban* and *dagnyas* could assure me there would be no more fights between the clans. They had my punishment, now it was up to them to sort the matter out by their own laws.

Having told them this, I turned and walked away, wondering if anyone would try to follow, wondering if another weapon would be aimed my way. Nobody followed and nothing was thrown.

I went down to the river to measure how much stone the women had collected and to tell them also to stop working and why. They dropped the stones they were carrying and headed for their encampment. Slowly the worksite emptied of people until there was just myself, Mike and Mohamed, who by this time was working as a gang foreman as much as being our translator.

Together we walked around collecting the discarded tools and checked them into the enclosure where they were normally stored. Amazingly every tool that had been checked out that morning was accounted for. I had wondered if any might have gone missing, particularly the machetes, but they were all there.

All this happened only an hour before our normal stopping time, so a reasonable amount of work had still been done that day. At the same time, it meant the loss to the people was all the greater for they had worked almost the whole day for nothing. On the way back to camp, I asked Mohamed to find the *makaban* and tell him I expected him to sort this out by his own rules, because it was really a tribal matter; I'd had my say back there by the rock.

IN THE MIDDLE of the afternoon, Tadese warned me there was a deputation approaching the camp. I asked him to make a vat of tea. It looked as if there was talking to be done and, by the number of people coming, it could go on for a long time. There must have been at least fifty people in the group, which was led by the *makaban* and all the Dodha elders. We sat down in the area under the trees that had become the regular talking place.

Doga Detolali told me the people had talked among themselves about what had happened but needed now to hear from me. From previous discussions and from Mohamed's explanations of how disputes of this sort were traditionally settled, I knew what to expect and told him, clearly enough for everyone present to hear, what I thought had happened.

I explained my concern that the man's chanting might be stirring up disagreement between the clans and that I wanted to take him aside to ask him to stop. I explained that all the clans were considered equal in our work and everyone would have an equal share of any crops that were eventually grown. I explained the need to work together so that the system was built in time to catch the rain from the mountains when it came down the *wadi*; any delay made this more difficult. Lastly I told them how I had reached out to take the man's wrist in the Afar way but he had raised his shovel and hit me with it.

Everyone listened carefully and nobody said a thing. I repeated the punishment that I had given for the offence, explaining how everyone had suffered the loss of a day's food tomorrow as a result, while those who had been involved would also lose the food they had earned for today's work. Now it was up to the tribe to use their own laws and make sure this never happened again. If it did, the work and the food that came with it would be finished and famine would return. I did not want that to happen.

The *dagnyas* huddled round the *makaban* and talked quietly together for several minutes and then asked me if the man who had started the fight was present now. I looked round the group carefully, not really expecting to see him. I fully expected that he would have headed off into the desert, leaving others to sort out the mess. But he was there, near the back of the crowd that had grown to about ninety people and now included women and children as well as the men.

I told them the man was present.

"What is his name?" the *makaban* asked.

By this time I knew many of our workers by name, but this man was a relative newcomer and I hadn't learned his. I went over, stood in front of him and asked, *"Ku miga iya?"*

"Yi miga Ali Waré," he replied.

I went back to the *makaban* and told him, "The man tells me he is called Ali Waré."

The elders consulted quietly again, then summoned Ali Waré. They told him he was guilty of starting the fight and causing other people to suffer. They told him he must apologise and that he was fined his two best sheep, the best one to be given to me and the other one to the tribe, who would eat it.

With no word of argument, Ali Waré calmly took off his sandals and laid them aside. He took off his *ga'abi*, folded it and placed it on top of the sandals. Then he unbuckled the knife at his waist and laid this on top of the *ga'abi*. He looked around at the crowd of people watching and walked over to the youngest, a boy of about five.

Touching the knuckles of his right hand to his own forehead then lips, he offered a loose fist to the boy and told him he was sorry for causing the fight. The boy reached out with his own right hand open, placed it over Ali Waré's hand and nodded. Then he moved on to the next person and repeated the same apology. Each person briefly covered the offered fist with their own hand and nodded acceptance. And so it went on, around the whole assembly, children, women and men alike in ascending order of seniority until, after almost half an hour, he came to the *makaban* and to me. Now he knelt on the ground to offer his apology whereas before he had merely stooped.

I was the last and Mohamed had warned me that I would need to respond. After that Ali Waré would bring the sheep he had been fined.

He kissed his knuckles and offered me the hand saying clearly the humiliating words of apology. I took his hand and held it a moment before I spoke.

"I accept your apology Ali Waré and I accept that the judgement is fair. You have had my punishment for the offence and that matter was ended then. Now you have the punishment of your own people and all can see it is just. When we resume work in two days' time, do you wish to work peacefully with everyone else and earn food for your work?"

"I wish to work," he said.

"Then come on the morning that work starts again and I will write your name in the book. Now this matter is ended, so let's have no more arguments or fights on the worksite." I let go of his hand.

Ali Waré picked up his *gillé* and buckled it round his waist, he draped his *ga'abi* round his shoulders, put his feet in his sandals and shuffled off, leaving the meeting seated.

Tadese had been passing out tins of tea while the talking was going on. Many of the Afar had brought mugs and cups they had been given from the goods Tefera had delivered a few weeks before. More tea was distributed now and a low rumble of conversation started as we waited.

Ten minutes later Ali Waré returned. He was carrying a sheep over his shoulders and leading another by a short rope tied round its horns. He presented the one he was carrying to me and the other to the *makaban*, who asked for his knife also. Ali Waré drew his *gillé* and handed it to Doga. The *makaban* wasted no time slaughtering the sheep and then called for someone to light a fire and cook it. He returned the knife to its owner and told him to skin the sheep.

I didn't know what I was going to do with a sheep; I certainly didn't have time to take it out to graze each day. These were not big animals and one was surely not going to be enough to feed all the people who had assembled. I suggested to Doga that he should kill this one as well, so that everyone could eat well.

"You kill it," he said. "It was paid to you so you must kill it if it is to be eaten."

"But the people won't eat it if I kill it," I said. "I am considered *nasrani*; they will require it to be killed by a Muslim."

"They will eat it," he said and called Ali Waré to bring his knife and let me dispatch the sheep.

There was a sudden hush as I took the knife and tested its inner edge to make sure it was sharp. I wasn't aware of hesitating, but Ali Waré said, "Kill it, they will eat your meat."

I was aware that everyone was watching to see how I would do the deed, but this didn't bother me. It was something I had done many times before as I had long been accustomed to buying my meat on the hoof or to shooting it. Now, with a sharp knife it was easy to do cleanly and in a few seconds I was opening the skin and peeling it back from the carcass as the blood drained into a hollow scooped out of the ground. In less than ten minutes, the carcass was prepared for cooking and handed over to those in charge of the fire. The other animal, although it had been killed first, was still being cleaned. I pegged out the skin on the ground to stretch and dry, giving the head and lungs to a boy to take out into the bush and leave for the evening scavengers. After that I cleaned and twisted the intestines into a long cord that would later have many uses.

As I sat down, Doga leaned over and told me the way I'd done the job had earned many favourable comments. That wasn't why I'd done it, but I was pleased my actions had met with approval. The last few hours had been tense and every bit as much a trial for me as for the man who had caused the trouble. But at least now it looked as if we might be able to put it behind us. I wondered how things would be when work resumed.

16 ~ Trouble with invaders

DAWN ON THE DAY work restarted was sultry and overcast. In any other part of Africa, with a different society, this might have been taken as an omen. Here it was just an inconvenience. The early wind felt heavy and more dust-laden than usual but the heat didn't increase as rapidly as on days when the desert sun scorched us.

Queues of workers were already forming before it was fully light and I soon realised that more people than usual were there. This was encouraging as numbers had been growing too slowly and I was beginning to be concerned about how to attract more. Now everyone wanted to work and there were so many new faces that I knew very few of them. Why had they suddenly become so keen to join in?

Ali Waré presented himself and I wrote his name in the book as I had promised. I handed him a shovel and asked him to go back to the same spot to continue the work that had been interrupted, following a few minutes later to see how things were going. He and the others in the group were shaving the sloping side of the main channel to match the gradient board. I was pleased to see that although Ali Waré was doing a lot of talking, he was also working well. This time his talk was instructing the others how to use their tools correctly and making sure that they didn't dig too deep and spoil the slope. He obviously understood quite well what we were doing and I began to wonder if I might have found a potential new foreman.

But it was the other things I heard him saying that interested me. He was telling the other men that they had to work hard now because a *nasrani* would never respect the Afar laws the way I had and therefore I must understand what Allah wanted the same way they did. The judgement had been just and it must be respected, so they should listen and work. That way everyone would get food. His words surprised me.

Listening to some of the talk as I walked around, I overheard another man telling his friends who had been discussing the incident and how I had handled it, "No, he's not a Christian. The Christians don't think like that. He respects our laws; he must be one of us, but with a white skin." Had Ali Waré already spoken to this man or was this a general view? Whatever it was, it seemed to have boosted morale tremendously, so I took it as a compliment.

TWO DAYS LATER a group of people arrived in a state of high agitation. They had been camped a few miles away but so far none of their group had come to join the work. The previous night they had been attacked by an Issa raiding party who crossed the border from Somalia. All their goats had been stolen. They hadn't had many goats and only one camel, but that, along with one of their men, had been killed. As the Issa drove their animals away, the three men and eight women had fled to the safety of our camp in search of help.

Encounters between the Afar and Issa were invariably brief,

hostile, bloody and likely to result in fatalities which ensured the continuance of a feud that had endured for generations. So deep did the animosity run that as recently as the 1950s, the Afar continued to mutilate the bodies of dead Issa raiders by cutting off their testicles and, after drying, wearing them as a necklace for a year of more. Only when they met on neutral ground, principally in the enclave of Djibouti, did the enemies rub along without actually fighting very often.

Taking one of the men in the Land Rover, I went back to where their camp had been. Three *a'aris* had been burned and lay as smouldering ash heaps. The crude stock pen, roughly torn apart, showed clear tracks where their herd had been driven off at speed. The slaughtered camel, fly blown and already starting to smell, lay in the dust nearby. A fresh mound of earth surrounded with a rough ring of stones marked where the dead member of the family had been hastily buried.

We walked around the desolate camp for a few minutes and picked up everything which might still have a use that had been dropped or overlooked when they fled. Then I drove to the nearest *wadi* and collected a large pile of flat stones in the back of the Land Rover. These we placed neatly over the grave to stop hyenas and other scavengers digging it up after they had disposed of the camel. Using my sextant, I fixed the position of the camp. Then we left.

Back at our own camp, I wrote a detailed report of what had happened and addressed it to both the District Governor and the Enderassie, asking for action to guard the frontier against these incursions. I took it down to Fred's bar. As luck would have it, a tanker stood by the roadside. The driver agreed, for a small fee, to take my letter.

The following day, Tefera arrived on the worksite to make his own investigation into what had happened. I got the man who had accompanied me to the destroyed camp to guide the governor back there himself, with Mohamed to translate for them as Tefera didn't speak Afar and the local man had no Amharic. Two hours later they were back. Tefera told me he had sent my report on to the Enderassie and would now follow it with his own. He would ask for frontier guards but didn't expect much support. I got the impression that he had a very low opinion of our provincial Governor General and wondered if he might have been one of the clique of Rases who had once condemned Tefera to prison. There was evidently no friendship between the two now and not much respect either.

Two days later, we heard of another raid by the Issa. This time they had come across the Chelaka River, right where Bruce and I had surveyed only a few months before. Nobody had been killed but the Abu Sama'ara clan who lived in the area had all decamped and moved further north.

I sent another report but once again the Enderassie took no notice. Nobody was sent to ensure the security of the border. Either he just didn't believe the Issa had come or he didn't care. A similar report to the LMB produced no reaction whatsoever. I had no way of knowing who had received it but either they didn't take the matter seriously or else, as I now thought probable, Ato Abaye had intercepted and suppressed it. I still didn't understand why he wanted our project to fail, but had been told twice on the grapevine that he had actually announced this to a number of reliable people. I wondered what part he played in the political undercurrent I had been observing.

17 ~ Dryer, hotter, wetter

SINCE WORK HAD STARTED, we kept simple meteorological records on a daily basis. When Tadese joined the team, he was fascinated by the equipment, so I taught him how to take the readings and delegated the observation and record keeping to him. He was always in camp and he proved to be reliable, taking pride in keeping neat records of accurate readings. We measured maximum and minimum temperatures every twenty-four hours, daily temperature at dawn, lunch time and dusk and relative humidity along with wind velocity and direction.

By mid-May, the temperature was peaking at over 148 degrees Fahrenheit at one o'clock, which was why that was when work stopped. It generally subsided to a low of about a hundred degrees overnight. The humidity hadn't been much above ten per cent for several months, even on those recent days when the sky had been full of heavy low clouds. The desert plants were parched and desiccated; only the few tomatoes and spinach in our garden showed any green. Small dust devils regularly skittered across the bare ground, driven by the hot wind which sucked the moisture out of everything. The few animals which had survived the

MET READINGS

WENANZO. May 1974

Date	1	2	3	MAX	MIN	RH	WD	WS
1	106	138	135	144	102	9		
2	111	135	137	146	101	9	E	8
3	109	138	129	145	102	6	E	10
4	106	140	135	145	102	10	E	9
5	107	141	137	144	103	9	SE	10
6	104	142	132	146	106	5	SE	5
7	105	141	130	144	102	5	E	12
8	108	140	133	144	101	4	SE	10
9	103	141	137	147	104	5	E	12
10	101	144	138	146	100	8	SE	8
11	102	145	140	148	102	7	E	6
12	103	145	139	146	100	8	-	-
13	101	146	141	148	103	6	SE	8
14	100	147	140	148	103	5	SE	12
15	101	145	139	146	100	7	SE	6
16	102	147	141	149	101	4	-	0
17	100	147	140	147	102	5	-	0
18	102	146		146	103	5	-	1-2

Temperatures peaked daily above 140 degrees, sapping energy.

drought looked listless and shrunken, wearing skins that appeared too big for them. The people too looked shrivelled and lethargic, doing everything in slow motion without any energy despite the good food they were now receiving.

There was little grazing in our area and many men had divided their families, sending the younger members elsewhere with their sheep and goats in the hope that they might find better pasture. The water holes that had existed a few months ago were now virtually dry and even the well I dug had dried out to a mere puddle at the bottom. I put a probe down to see if it was worth digging deeper but the reservoir I had tapped was depleted and would not hold water again until any seasonal flows from the mountains refilled it.

ANOTHER INFESTATION of locusts had been discovered a few hundred yards from the weir and this time a message was sent to Tefera asking for help. It was our good fortune that messages sent to him generally resulted in action and a few days later a locust eradication officer arrived. He came in a battered Land Rover with tanks of insecticide and a backpack sprayer. He spent three days walking round spraying every location where locusts had been found, or where he suspected they might have laid eggs. He took no notice of the Afar and they took no notice of him; he concerned himself solely with his own task from dawn to dusk and slept in the back of his old Land Rover.

We had two cloudless days following the locust man's visit and the temperature soared, reaching 154 degrees on the hottest day. Even with the humidity at only four per cent, this was so uncomfortable we stopped work two hours early but still paid everyone for a full day's work.

On the third day, we woke to find the sky low and sombre, full of heavy grey clouds. Their lower surface was roiling like bubbling soup as they scudded along on a stronger wind than usual, driving in from the east. The air was heavy, hot and unusually sticky. By ten o'clock it started raining. Everyone stopped what they were doing, dropping their tools to stand and look skyward.

Rain was something unknown to almost all the Afar working

on the site. Only the oldest had ever seen rain before. That had been so long ago in their childhood that it was now little more than a dim and uncertain memory. Farasabba Mohamed was one of these. On a previous occasion when he and I had discussed rain, we had calculated that it was fifty-seven years since it had last rained in this part of the desert. The Afar said there were occasional night mists at this time of the year, when dew sometimes condensed to give the *tribulus* plants and a few of the grasses an occasional brief flush of life, but this event was so different it felt like the onset of Noah's flood.

This idea was not surprising really as the rain got steadily heavier. In a few minutes, the soft dusty soil turned to thin squishy mud. People were slipping and sliding as they tried to walk and everyone soon began hurrying for shelter. Instead of blowing dust swirls in our faces as it normally did, the erratic wind now carried wet gusts of stinging raindrops which had people covering their faces with folds of their *ga'abis* as they stumbled for the cover of their *a'aris*.

It rained solidly for almost four hours. Even after the main downpour ceased, occasional showers continued until after dark. At dusk the sky was still obscured by clouds and darkness overtook us even more rapidly than usual. One moment it was grey, damp daylight, the next it was night. That night there was no cascade of sparkling stars to bathe the countryside in soft silver light, no rising moon to show late grazers the way back to their stock pens and their families.

Despite the rain, we spent the afternoon collecting dropped tools and checking the amount of soil that had been excavated from the diggings before the rain filled our excavations and turned them into pools. It was awhile since any of us had driven at night

Campsite after the rain: a slippery surface.

and we found that only one headlight worked on the Land Rover we had taken to the worksite that morning. It cast a baleful light on the mess as we steered cautiously between the camel thorn bushes on the way back to camp. The wheels rapidly became clogged with mud and even four-wheel drive did little to improve our ability to move across the slippery countryside.

The greasy texture of the surface started me thinking about the soil and I resolved to conduct more tests once this dried out. It appeared possible that we might have overlooked something during the original survey which could be important later. For the first time since we started, I found myself wondering if this project was really viable. Was there another confounding reason why the Afar had never adopted cultivation? Something in the soil?

MORNING BROUGHT a scene of complete desolation. The clouds had dispersed overnight leaving the sky a clear crystal blue dome overhead, clearer and brighter than we had ever seen it. The countryside was transformed with lakes of grey mud glistening in the early sunlight. Out of these stuck the spindly forms of spiny thorn bushes.

I sent word through the Afar encampment that there would be no work until the land had dried out but that everyone would still be paid for the days we didn't work; all they had to do was turn up and get their names checked off. After all the privation of the drought, it would be unfair if nature deprived them of their food a second time now that they had got the idea of earning it.

There was no point in trying to use the Land Rover, so I walked back to the site that morning, stopping every few yards to scrape the accumulating clods of mud off my shoes. One or two of the Afar came too, curious to see how much of their efforts had been destroyed. Among them was Ali Waré who, unasked, helped collect the last of tools from where they had been dropped when the rain started and stack them in piles in the tool pen. We walked around the site together and looked at the destruction.

Most of the loose soil had been washed away and the shape of the banks looked different today. It was clear that the river had carried a strong flow during the night and it was still full of water, although this was moving only sluggishly now. The four large heaps of stones which had been placed ready to fill the weir gabions were now spread out but most were still reasonably nearby. Of the gabion baskets which had been opened and assembled ready for filling, there was no sign. We still had a supply waiting for the next layer, ready stacked on the bank, so losing the bottom layer would only delay us a little and they could soon be replaced. We were expecting more gabions anyway because we had ordered more when I discovered Ato Abaye had interfered with the original consignment. He would enjoy the fact

River once more: the shelf cut into the bank to accommodate the takeoff was largely undamaged by the deluge.

that we needed to order more again and no doubt he would somehow use this as an opportunity for further obstruction.

Surprisingly, the shelf that had been cut into the river bank to accommodate the takeoff from the weir was relatively undamaged. A few days' work would soon see that put right. In addition, almost all the marker pegs that Mike had put out remained where he had placed them. The tops protruded like little stubs from the glistening sea of slick mud.

There was not much we could do on the site until it dried out, so we went back to camp. We dug the accumulated mud from the Land Rover's wheel arches and set off for Fred's bar to see how the people in the village had fared during the storm. The going was slow and it took twice as long as usual to get there. The usual track was under water in many places and the two *wadis* we had to cross were now three feet deep in water.

Over the next few days, the land dried out. Slowly it returned to the same parched, dusty state it was in before the rain. More gabions arrived and work started again. As soon as the river bed had dried enough, a new trench was dug across it and a twin line of gabions for the weir foundation was placed, laced together and filled. Work on the channel was soon proceeding apace, but it was still too slow for what was needed and time was getting short. As things were, if rain fell in the mountains when it should, we would not be ready. For a few days we agonised over what to do and eventually agreed to bring in a mechanical digger. Once again Ato Abaye tried to change the arrangements and we had to go to the mountains and organise it ourselves.

Slowly something resembling an irrigation system began to emerge from the chaos. Provided we did get flow down the *wadi* when the monsoon hit the mountains, it just might be possible to plant a crop. Morale among the Afar was improving as the work proceeded. This was in part because they could see the results of their labours but also because they were now in much better physical condition. With regular food they were no longer suffering so acutely from the effects of the drought, although the lack of clean water was still an issue.

SOMEONE SENIOR IN THE LMB hierarchy in Addis Ababa was keen that at least two sites should be involved in the project. It must have been somebody much more senior than Ato Abaye as he would surely have done something to prevent it had he been able to. But he remained mute. At the beginning, we had proposed an alternative use for the Chelaka River site, so I was asked to revisit that area and talk to the tribes about working there. Work was now far enough advanced and going smoothly at Weranzo, so it was time to do something about this. I handed over to Mike, packed my bag and headed for the village.

Everything in the village looked damp and drab. Fred complained that his roof had leaked badly and the pyramid of useless grain had subsided into a soggy round hump. Otherwise, apart from some muddy water standing in the ditches on either side of the road, there was little evidence that anything had happened.

There was other news, however. The Issa had made another raid; this time on a family camped only a few miles south of the road.

There was still no sign of any help arriving from the authorities in Dessie and I began to think we would have to do something ourselves. While I was at Fred's bar, more news came in. A dozen or more Issa were heading south towards the border driving a large flock they had accumulated.

I didn't stay long in the village but headed towards Eliwoha to talk to the Abu Sama'ara. This time I had no trouble finding either the *makaban* or his *balabat*. Despite the news about the Issa, they were both amenable to my proposition and agreed to visit the Chelaka River with me to discuss what I wanted to do.

18 ~ Sickness at Eliwoha

BEFORE WE COULD GO anywhere, a man from one of the *a'aris* on the edge of the village came over asking for help for his sick brother. This cluster of *a'aris* was already familiar as it had been here that I had met and treated the women affected by the bad smallpox vaccine. Mike and I had made numerous visits to clean and dress the wounds and usually stopped every time we passed through Eliwoha, to see if things were improving. Most of the wounds were healing slowly but eight of the older women had died since the problem first came to light. I had helped dig at least six of their graves and the cluster of stone-covered *wadella*, three hundred yards to the north, had grown from six to several dozen. New ones were still being added every few days.

The man led me to an *a'ari* that had not been here last time I came. Two younger women were seated outside and an older woman was inside, tending a man who was prostrate in the gloom. She came out as we approached and the man led me forward to meet his brother.

The man inside looked grey and listless. He was obviously in great discomfort. His brother said he had an open wound but at first this was not obvious, although the smell of rotting flesh was. It was only when he lifted the cloth draped over his brother's body that the problem became apparent. Raw flesh covered the man's lower abdomen, shocking pink, suffused with pus and scabs. This was not a new wound; it had been there for some time and large patches of flesh had been eaten away. His penis looked as if something had taken a bite out of it and the front half of his scrotum had gone, leaving his testicles raw and exposed. Flies descended as soon as the wound was exposed and the smell in the stuffy little shelter made me retch.

It wasn't possible to see the full extent of the wound in that cramped space, especially since I was blocking out most of the light by crouching in the doorway, so I asked the brother to move the man out into the daylight while I went to my Land Rover and brought the first aid kit and other supplies.

Bringing him into the daylight revealed just how serious the

Funeral at Eliwoha: the piles of stones mark other recent graves.

Fresh graves at Eliwoha, a stark reminder of drought's price.

man's injury was. He needed far more help than I could give so I asked him if he was willing to come with me to Bati where I would find a doctor to treat him. I should have known better than to expect a yes or no answer; he was an Afar. This question, like everything else, became the subject of an intense discussion centred around who would look after his family and his goats while he was gone. Eventually, with the brother's encouragement and reassurance from everyone else present, he agreed to come with me.

I went back to the *makaban* and told him our expedition to the Chelaka River would have to be postponed for a few days while I took the man to get medical attention. Neither he nor the *balabat* had any objection to this but both immediately asked to accompany us to Bati. At first it looked as if they were being supportive, but it soon became apparent that they just wanted a ride to the town to visit friends in the market.

The trip to Bati must have been purgatory for Aliamu Hamid, as the *makaban* told me the injured man was called, but he sat beside me, uncomplaining, as we bumped our way over the poorly maintained section of the road. Before tackling the steep incline up the escarpment, we paused at the spring for a few minutes to drink fresh water and to refill the plastic water container that lived in the Land Rover. I had used most of its twenty-five litres back in Eliwoha to clean Aliamu's wound.

It was late afternoon when we stopped at the relief camp. As luck would have it, we were met just inside the gate by an English doctor, Robert Foster, who agreed at once to have a look at the patient when I explained why we had come. His face showed utter dismay when he saw what we had brought him.

"How long has he been like this?" he asked.

"About three months," I said because it was a question I had already asked Aliamu.

"Wow, and I bet it hurts," the doctor observed, gently probing around the outer edges of the raw flesh. "Well, there's not much I can do with this except pile drugs into him and hope to stop whatever it is that's eating his flesh. The testicles and most of his penis will have to go, I'm afraid, but we should be able to keep him alive."

The suggestion horrified me and I didn't translate it to the patient.

"You can't do that to him, he's an Afar," I protested. "Haven't you heard what they do to their enemies?"

He hadn't, having been in the country only six weeks and never having met any Afar. I explained and told him that, succeed or fail, he'd have to offer something that didn't involve removing the man's marriage tackle.

He thought for a few minutes, then said Aliamu would have to stay at the camp and sit in a bowl of disinfectant several times every day, swallow a lot of pills and receive a few injections. They would feed him, look after him and tend his wound and I could come back in a few weeks and see if they had made any progress. That was the best he could offer.

It wasn't ideal, but at least he was willing to try. I explained to Aliamu and asked him if he would stay.

The doctor had given him some strong pain killers at the beginning of his examination and these had already begun to take effect. With the pain diminished he felt better and thought he ought to go home. Somebody was needed to look after his goats and his wives.

I was staggered that even this was going to turn into a negotiation! Did these Afar never do anything without a protracted argument first?

We had come directly to the camp so the *makaban* and the *balabat* were still sitting in the Land Rover. I explained Aliamu's concerns and asked them to help persuade him. They didn't want to discuss anything as they were keen to go and visit their friends, so they told him they would ensure that his goats and family were cared for and would be exactly where he had left them when I brought him home in a few weeks time.

At last Aliamu agreed and Dr Foster took him to a hut where he was seated in a bowl of disinfectant and given some food. Before leaving, I told him I would come back in a few days and see how he was getting on, promising to bring him news of his goats and his family. As a last thing I asked him to promise to remain in the camp and let the doctor treat him until I came back.

Reluctantly he gave his word.

Not far from the camp was a military-looking set-up with two camouflaged helicopters parked outside. It was the German markings that made me pause as I drove past the fence. Then I remembered that at one of the relief committee meetings in Dessie, a German delegate had told me there was a *Bundesgrenzschutz* team here which included medics. These were Federal German frontier guards, who had been involved since early in the emergency. With the greater mobility their helicopters gave them, they might be able to offer a bit of medical assistance to the Afar. I went in to ask. There was nobody in their camp at that moment who could make such a decision, but the clerk took down all the details, including location coordinates of our worksite. He said he would pass them on and I could call in tomorrow if I was in town. If not, he promised someone would be in contact within a week. There was no alternative but to leave it at that, but it had been worth trying.

I took the *makaban* and *balabat* to visit their friends in the market and since it was getting dark, suggested I would pick them up early in the morning and we would go then to look at the Chelaka River. At the hotel, I had a long shower, a meal of bean soup and *injera*, and slept soundly until morning.

19 ~ The Chelaka sand dam

WHEN WE HAD ORIGINALLY surveyed the Chelaka River, it had been obvious that the best place to build a weir was where the river channel was narrowed by rock outcrops on each bank with a distinct drop in the river bed below. Construction was complicated by the necessity for cutting through the side of one of these outcrops and along a rock shelf to make a channel between the weir and the fields. On that side of the river, the rock was covered by only a few inches of topsoil so this would be a major engineering task, requiring either heavy equipment or explosives to excavate any sort of channel.

The whole ethos of the project was to achieve our aim using only manual labour and simple technology, so this put the place beyond further consideration for use as an irrigation site. We had already had to compromise at Weranzo by bringing in a digger to help excavate the long channel, but at least that site was accessible. Here it would be totally impractical without first building a road, and that level of work was not justified.

We had left the Chelaka River for future development in the hope that more funds could be found for a future project as

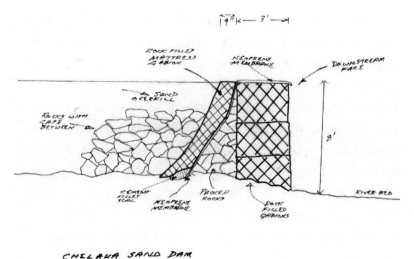

CHELAKA SAND DAM
STRUCTURE

something might still be possible. But there was another option that fell within the terms of the current programme.

The alternative was to create a sand dam. This would produce a protected reservoir and assure a good supply of stored water, even in the driest conditions. The principle was a simple one I had already used successfully several times in West Africa. It involved blocking the river channel completely with an impervious wall and piling large rocks up behind it to just below the level of the obstruction. A layer of smaller stones and finally sand on top of this would fill the river bed upstream of the wall for several hundred yards. Water flowing down the channel would accumulate behind the barrier, filling the spaces between the rocks until eventually it spilled over the top. Because the storage area was covered by sand, the water would not evaporate in the summer heat, but could be drawn from wells at the side for people and livestock. Simple drinking troughs into which it could be poured were easy enough to build.

When we arrived at the site, I made a small model to explain to the *makaban* and the *balabat* what I proposed. It didn't take either of them long to understand the value of this idea. They agreed to gather their people here in two weeks so we could talk about it. They had heard all about the food-for-work programme near Weranzo. Although the Abu Sama'ara people had now received some relief supplies, they were envious that the Dodha tribe seemed to be getting something they were not. The opportunity to earn food had many attractions and since their herds had been more completely depleted by the drought than those of some other tribes, the idea became all the more attractive.

I HAD RECEIVED instructions relating to my other assignment so a delay before the talking began gave me a good opportunity to go into the mountains and follow that up. I also wanted to go back and see how Aliamu was in the Bati camp.

When I got to the town, I found another task waiting for me; one which involved a British children's television programme. *Blue Peter* had been collecting money to replace oxen that had died because of the drought. The animals were used by a Galla village a few miles south-west of Kombolcha. New oxen were now ready for delivery but the programme's managers needed to be sure that there would be enough water along the delivery route and in the recipient village to sustain them. For some reason that was never explained, our director had volunteered my services for this and, since the oxen's arrival was imminent and was to be filmed, action was needed without delay.

I visited the village and found two undeveloped springs which, with a little work, could be adapted to provide a generous water supply. They had never dried completely during the drought but the water had been trickling away down cracks in the rock and was lost to the villagers, who didn't know how to catch it. Along the mountain track leading to the village there were several damp patches which offered potential as watering points.

Negotiation with the Galla headman and his elders was a much more straightforward business than it had been with the Afar and it did not take long to agree a course of action. Since the director had committed me to the task, I assumed she was also going to pick up the tab for any materials the project needed, so I ordered them, arranged for them to be dropped off at the nearest point on the road, and had the bill sent to the development attaché at the Embassy. The headman brought a team of mules to transport everything to where it was needed along the winding mountain paths. Many of these had a sheer five-hundred-foot drop on one side and walking along them after the flat expanse of the desert was an unnerving experience.

The villagers waiting to receive the oxen were quick to understand what was required and willing to work hard, so things soon began to happen. We were halfway through building a collecting box at one spring when a *Blue Peter* film crew turned up. They were a merry bunch who spent a lot of time getting in the way and not much time shooting film, but they were also happy to join in and do a bit of labouring. After a few days they went off to film the oxen, which were being brought from a different part of the country not affected by the drought.

I WENT BACK to the desert while they were doing that and talked to the Abu Sama'ara about the sand dam project. The stream, which had still contained a small trickle of water when Bruce and I surveyed the site, was now almost dry, with less than

The wide Chelaka riverbed with barely a trickle of water in it.

a gallon a minute dribbling over the hot rocks. Very few standing pools remained and the local herdsmen were finding it increasingly difficult to water their stock.

Once again my model proved its worth. I had made a new one on a board, which actually retained water behind the dam. This could be seen in a small well at the side of the miniature river bed. Drawing thimblefuls of water out of the minute well provided a very real demonstration which everyone understood. It took only one day's discussion to agree everything, which showed how keen these people were to get involved and earn some food.

During the three visits I had made to the river, my Land Rover had carved a narrow track though a belt of dense thorn scrub on the slope above the river valley. Before leaving to arrange the delivery of supplies, I asked the Afar to clear enough of the thorn bushes along the track to make it wide enough so that a lorry bringing the materials could come along it. After the supplies were brought in, we would use the same lorry to transport the people and all their possessions as well. This they soon agreed. The Afar would be able to use the wood from the cut acacias for their cooking fires if they tied it into bundles, as these too could be piled into the lorry and brought to the site.

I was presuming a lot in promising this and hoped Tefera would cooperate as I had in mind to use one of his lorries and had yet to ask his permission. In the event, he saw the sense of it and agreed immediately. Having had several sessions with the Abu Sama'ara *balabat*, Tefera told me he was one of the more cooperative ones who still had some influence over the tribe he represented. Many of the others did nothing except draw their government salary and sit around being difficult; no use to either their people or the government that had appointed them.

IN THE BATI CAMP, I found Aliamu sitting in his bowl of disinfectant, looking gloomy and sad. His wound looked surprisingly good and the infection was now under control. New skin was growing over his abdomen and around the raw edges of his scrotum. But he wasn't happy and he didn't want to stay there. We talked for some time and I explained how important it was that he should stay a few more weeks as the doctor's work was producing a good result.

Aliamu still wasn't happy, even though he knew what I was saying was true. The truth was he missed his goats and his family. I offered to bring his wives up to see him, but still he insisted he wanted to go home. I finally persuaded him to stay one more week and then, if the doctor said it was all right, I would take him home to see them. He was satisfied with this so I left him there again.

20 ~ Ambush

MATERIALS ARRIVED AT the Chelaka River and a number of Afar families took advantage of my offer of transport and moved down to a spot close by. Just as I expected, more discussion was necessary before any work could begin. This time it was about the amount of food people would be paid for working.

We had only just concluded our discussions when news came in about another Issa raid. This one had happened only about twenty miles away, directly to the south of us. Given the way the land lay, it was clear that if the Issa came any further north, they would have to come right through here.

As all my requests for action had been ignored, it was abundantly clear that the Ethiopian authorities had no intention of doing anything about this menace. It was up to us to do something for ourselves.

For some time I had been considering a radical plan. It wasn't likely to make me popular with the authorities and would almost certainly be vetoed by the Embassy if they knew of it, but they weren't here and I was. The news of this new raid hardened my resolve, so I headed east along the main road in the direction of

Assayita, where the Afar Sultan lived. If no help was forthcoming from the government, I would find some myself. Surely the sultan would be willing to assist his own people.

I had met Sultan Ali Mirah before. He was a round, jovial man who listened patiently and with great interest while I explained the problem. He spread his hands and said he could not offer me any men to prevent the Issa coming. All his people were as badly off as everyone else, despite being near the big Mitchell Cotts agricultural enterprise at Dubti, with secure water and food supplies. He did, however, agree to lend me some weapons so that our people could fight back and stop the Issa themselves. Taking me to a room in his rambling mud-walled palace, he showed me a pile of old Lee Enfield Mk I rifles, dating from the First World War, and told me to pick out a hundred. They were leaning against the wall in a huge pile and most had not seen gun oil in many a year. Someone had, however, had the foresight to spread a canvas sheet over them to keep off the worst of the dust and pigeon droppings. To go with the rifles he sold me two thousand rounds of ammunition for a hundred dollars, but warned me some of it might not be very good as it had once got damp. The price was cheap, so I didn't argue. With his help freely given like this, that would have been churlish.

Taking my haul back to Eliwoha, I recruited ten more men from the village and took them down to join their friends and relations at the Chelaka River. There, in between periods of work on the dam, I taught them how to shoot straight and how to lay ambushes. Growing up in an army family proved, for once, to have an advantage as I had seen my father train other African troops to do this same thing. Most of them knew their own countryside well and they soon got the idea. Next time the Issa came, we would steer them into a trap. We sent out scouts to make sure we got early word when they came again, as we knew they surely would. Then we got on with building the dam.

THE RECENT RAIN HAD brought about a dramatic change to the countryside. Within twenty-four hours, most of the water had either vanished into the soil or evaporated and the desert had changed colour. Millions of thorny *tribulus* seeds, which might have lain dormant for dozens of years, germinated and almost immediately turned the desert green. Within thirty-six hours, the little plants spread out to cover every open patch of soil with a dense green mat of delicate bi-pinnate leaves. The following morning these plants erupted into a mass of tiny yellow flowers, turning the desert floor from fresh green to a vivid primrose yellow. The early morning wind helped spread the pollen, released almost as soon as the flowers opened, and by nightfall the first seeds were forming.

The plants grew at tremendous speed, germinating, flowering and fruiting before the relentless sun could scorch and burn them to a dried crisp. Within a few days all that remained were the dried straw coloured skeletons of the *tribulus* stems, bristling with thousands of small thorny seeds which would remain dormant until the next rain starts the cycle again.

While the *tribulus* were turning the desert floor green, the spiny acacia bushes, that were usually no more than thorn-laden sticks, now had a covering of feathery green leaflets. The bigger trees, near the river bank, suddenly burst into flower, wearing crowns of soft pink and gold. Even the desiccated grey clumps of old grass sprouted new growth.

Everyone was amazed; the Afar were jubilant. No longer

needing to drive their herds miles in search of food, they let their scrawny animals out to graze freely on this new bounty.

WE NOW HAD GUARDS posted around the worksite in case the raiders came, and other men positioned in the approaches who would fire a volley of shots if they saw any intruders. Slowly things got back to work but within a few days, when word spread that we were working again and issuing food, people started coming back. Some had moved away in fear of being raided; the presence of armed guards obviously did something to help restore their confidence.

We heard occasional rumours about Issa incursions but nothing definite, so I kept the troops working on the dam site, only issuing the rifles when they were needed for training and to teach the men how to care for them properly. They were collected after each training session and locked in the back of the Land Rover.

Three weeks later, the Issa raiders struck again. There were twelve of them this time and they followed the bait we had laid out. Our warning system worked and our fighters were all positioned and well concealed by the time the raiders reached our prepared ambush. Even so, the invaders fought hard. Two of them carried AK47 rifles, which at that time were almost unknown in the area. Even the Ethiopian army was not equipped with anything that modern. This made the battle a harder fight than we had hoped, but the ambush was well laid, the Afar did what they had been taught to do and in less than half an hour it was all over.

Nine Issa bodies were collected, together with three men who were badly injured but still alive. None of our own men received so much as a scratch. High on the success of their action, some of the Afar fighters were all for carrying out the traditional mutilation and emasculating all the Issa, but I persuaded them at least to leave the live ones intact. We would take them all, dead and alive, and present them to the Enderassie in Dessie. Perhaps this would be proof enough for him finally to recognise that there was a problem.

The bodies were stacked on the Land Rover's roof rack, with the three live ones on top, all tied on with a rope. Well-armed tribesmen filled the seats with their rifles and spears sticking out of the windows and we headed for the mountains. It was slow going with such a load and the vehicle felt slightly unstable with the extra weight on its roof. It was particularly precarious going round some of the sharp bends when we climbed the steep incline up to Bati. We stopped briefly in the town to tell Tefera what had happened and then continued on to the regional capital.

THE ACTION HAD TAKEN place in mid-afternoon and it was already quite late as we passed through Bati. The road onwards to Kombolcha and Dessie is slow and tortuous so it was after midnight when we came to a halt outside the gate of the Governor General's residence. The guard was unwilling to let us enter and said that nobody could go in until daylight.

His protests died when a dozen Afar, impatient with the delay, climbed out of the Land Rover and came to see what was going on. The sight of a band of wild looking tribesmen, all armed with rifles, *gillés* and spears was too much for him and his courage faltered. He opened the gate and vanished into the darkness inside. So we drove in, stopped in front of the main entrance, dumped all the bodies on the white stone steps leading up to the front door and then knocked until a sleepy doorman opened it. At first he looked confused when we demanded that he get the

Enderassie out of bed, but then he saw the bodies and fled. Another man appeared and tried to say that the Enderassie wasn't there, but a dozen armed Afar drawing their knives and advancing up the steps soon persuaded him otherwise and he too disappeared inside.

When the Enderassie came down and saw what we had brought him, he was shocked but trying to maintain his composure. As he watched, one of the Afar drew his *gillé* and calmly sliced the testicles from one of the three live Issa. The Enderassie vomited. With none of his own guards in evidence, looking ill and frightened for his own safety, he promised to send troops that same day to secure the frontier.

We left the bodies on his doorstep as a reminder, climbed back into the Land Rover and drove off. I knew that with this I had clocked up a whole bucketful of black marks and it might not be long before the Ethiopian authorities asked me to leave, but I wasn't finished yet. There was still work to be done in the desert and since the Afar had kept faith with me, I didn't want to let them down. If the wheels of authority turned at their normal speed, it should be able to complete what I had been sent to do before any repercussions manifested themselves.

Deciding that I might as well have the whole sheep as the lamb before leaving Dessie, I drove to one of the big government-run relief stores to see what they had available that might help the Abu Sama'ara. Two Bedford three-tonners were parked in the yard, both with their keys in the ignition. I discovered that the *balabat*, who had come with us, had long ago learned to drive. He seemed reasonably competent, so I reasoned he might just be capable of driving the Land Rover back to Bati while I drove a lorry. From the stores we selected the things we needed, filling one lorry. The guard on the warehouse gate had melted into the darkness in the same way that those at the palace had. Before leaving I left a list of what we had taken on the store manager's desk and signed it on the authority of the Danakil Irrigation Mission. We were back on the road long before dawn.

With early traffic moving on the road and an inexperienced driver behind me, going back was even slower than coming up to Dessie had been and it was late morning before we reached Bati. Calling once more at the governor's office, I told him what we had done and he laughed, rubbing his hands in enjoyment and offered one of his own drivers for the lorry. The *balabat* was relieved as he had been scared out of his wits on the mountain bends, but at least he had managed to keep on the road and had not hit anything.

THE FOLLOWING DAY we heard the sound of a labouring engine approaching the Chelaka valley. It took some time to arrive, obviously following the tracks we had made and having trouble crossing some of the gullies. After about half an hour, two army vehicles emerged from the thicket and stopped on the river bank near our camp. A crowd of soldiers began to disembark from the trucks. I stopped what I was doing at the sand dam and went to see what they wanted.

A young officer climbed down from the cab of one of the trucks introducing himself as Captain Tahwi Haile Mengistu. He informed me that he had orders from the Enderassie to come and protect my workers.

I asked if he knew where he was and where the Issa had been. He didn't. I asked if he had been given a specific location to position his troops. He hadn't. The orders had simply been to come down here and protect the Afar from raiding Issa and that I would tell him where they were. Eventually he produced quite a good map which gave me pause to wonder why maps like this had been denied to our mission from the beginning. This map would have made much of our early work a lot easier.

With the map spread out on my camp table, I showed the captain where we were and where the recent skirmish had taken place, where the Issa had come across the border and the three most likely routes that they would use in future. I suggested he retrace his tracks, go further along the road to a point I marked on his map and then take the easier route down to the border. He should be there well before dark.

Slightly embarrassed at being in the wrong place, he agreed and issued a stream of orders to his sergeant. Half an hour later, the troops climbed back into their vehicles and went back the way they had come. The rest of us got on with what we had been doing.

The big trees that lined the river bank produced a reasonable amount of shade in the Chelaka valley. Taking advantage of this, we were able to work longer each day than had been possible in the exposed Weranzo site. So, while we stopped for three hours during the hottest part of the day, we carried on again later as it began to cool. We were in the process of packing the first gabion to fill the gap between the rock outcrops and form the dam wall when news arrived that the soldiers had not gone down to the border. They had driven along the main road as far as the village of Mille and then stopped. They were now camped beside the road about half a mile from the village. This was more than fifty miles from the border – completely the wrong place.

The sun was setting as I pulled my Land Rover to a halt outside the soldiers' camp. In the dying light, it was difficult to see clearly so I took a torch from the dashboard tray and held it so that the beam illuminated my face as I climbed out of the vehicle, calling out loudly to ask for the captain.

That was when things went badly wrong. A nervous sentry let fly two rounds from his rifle. The first skimmed the inside of my left thigh and the second hit me squarely in the chest just below my left collar bone, sending me reeling backwards. I dropped the torch and yelled for the captain.

It turned out that the captain wasn't even in the camp. He had gone into the village in search of a whorehouse, but the sound of rifle shots soon brought him running. He was full of apologies. He bustled about looking for a first aid kit but found none. I had one in my Land Rover which he eventually found and applied a large field dressing to the hole in my chest. I put one on my leg myself.

After a brief enquiry about why he hadn't taken his troops directly down to the border and some vague answers from the captain, I finally convinced him to move and go to the right place, telling him that the Afar would soon let me know if he didn't and his commander would hear everything. Hastily he gave orders for his men to break camp and move out. Realising he had made a bad mistake and hoping to offset it by helping me now, he offered a driver to take me to hospital. The nearest medical help was in Bati at the relief camps and the nearest hospital was at Kombolcha, more than three and a half hours' drive away in daylight, more now that it was dark. The wound in my chest was beginning to hurt badly and I wasn't sure I had the stamina to drive any distance on my own, so I accepted, wondering if the driver was also supposed to spy on me and let the captain know if I talked to anyone in authority.

THE DRIVE WAS LONG, slow and painful, despite the fact that the army driver did his best to make good speed. He was a lorry driver, had never driven a Land Rover and was unfamiliar with the gears. He was also genuinely concerned that all the jolting about on the rough road might be making my wound worse and causing me more pain. I didn't care, breathing was becoming a little difficult and I simply wanted to get to qualified help as fast as possible. There's a pain barrier you pass through at a time like that and the discomfort no longer seems relevant. My attention was focussed on getting enough air into my lungs and staying alive.

The doctor at the Bati camp had gone to visit another camp and nobody knew what time he would be back; probably not until the morning. I decided not to hang about and told the driver to take me to the hospital in Kombolcha.

It was almost two in the morning by the time we finally reached the hospital. It was a rundown place with shabby walls in need of a coat of paint. There was a single dim lamp outside the front door and only a few lights along the dingy corridors inside. It took half an hour to locate the doctor, a Hungarian surgeon, who stumbled bleary-eyed from his bed smelling strongly of alcohol. He examined the wound, told me the bullet would have to be dug out and laid me on a table. There was no anaesthetic and the x-ray machine had been broken for months, so the only way he could find the bullet was by digging around inside my chest, probing with a long thin instrument. I hoped he had sterilised it.

After a few minutes of indescribable pain, he proudly held up the projectile. It was misshapen and bloody, but at least it was out. He packed the wound with sulphaguanidine powder and applied a dressing, reeling off barely intelligible instructions on how to care for it. He suggested I should take a strong antibiotic for five days, which I could get from a pharmacy in the town, and then simply walked out.

The worried driver helped me from the table and supported me as we went outside to the Land Rover. I had large tins full of antibiotic capsules down in my camp, so decided not to wait for the town's pharmacies to open. The best thing to do was to go back to Bati to rest for a few hours and get some food before going back to the desert. I also wanted to call on Tefera who would undoubtedly want to know what had happened as the soldiers were now in his territory.

21 ~ Setbacks, solutions, flow

IT WAS TWO DAYS BEFORE I got back to the Chelaka with one of Tefera's men driving. He had kept the army driver in Bati and instructed his own driver to remain with me until I was able to drive myself comfortably. He had also promised to visit in a few days and bring another load of food to pay the workers.

Word had somehow reached the worksite about what happened in Mille and the Abu Sama'ara had stopped work, uncertain about how to carry on. They understood perfectly well how to fill the gabions and there was no need to stop, but without leadership they seemed unwilling to do anything. I told them they didn't deserve to be fed if that was how they were going to behave, but issued the rations anyway. It wasn't worth an argument as I was still very sore and feeling off-colour. Work soon restarted.

The Abu Sama'ara had fewer animals than some of the other tribes and not many of these had been brought down to the Chelaka when their owners came to work on the sand dam. There were only a few goats, which gave a few pints of milk each day, and one camel in the communal stock pen beside the Afar encampment. They had set up their *a'aris* among the thorn bushes a few yards back from where my own tent was situated on the river bank and they drove their beasts past me each morning on their way down to the stream to drink. There were very few open watering places left now and we had needed to dig out one of the last remaining pools to accommodate them. Now they had to compete with a troop of baboons, a few gazelle and a solitary cheetah and its cub which lived in the area. The drought was again biting hard, although there had been a lot more clouds recently. If the season ran normally, these would soon increase, bringing monsoon rain in from the east to fall somewhere far to the west of us. Some days after that happened we might get a flow of water in this river bed again.

A week after the shooting incident, I was woken one night by the noise of a tremendous fight in the Afar encampment. Shots were fired and I feared the Issa had managed to sneak through and were making a night raid. After about ten minutes the noise settled down and tranquillity returned. Soon afterwards two men approached, one supporting the other, seeking help.

A gang of spotted hyenas had attacked the stock pen and one had managed to get inside, killing four of the goats and injuring the camel before someone shot it. While fighting off the marauders, a man called Agamé had collected a lot of lacerations on his legs from the thorn fence. Another man, Hamid Milliam, had managed to shoot himself in the leg while trying to shoot one of the hyenas. Happily the bullet had gone straight through his thigh muscle without tearing too big a hole and, although it hurt, he could still walk.

I got out the first aid kit and set to work.

Agamé's legs looked a mess. It took a long time to pick out the broken tips of the thorns and clean all the cuts and scratches.

Hamid's leg was not too bad and a few stitches and a couple of smart dressings were all that was needed, although I dosed both men with antibiotics to make sure no infection took hold.

Once again I was amazed by the stoicism of these men. I had used a little local anaesthetic when putting the stitches in, but the process couldn't have been without pain and yet neither flinched or complained, sitting patiently and watching as I worked.

Later that morning when we got back to work there was another problem: there was not enough galvanised wire for wiring the top mesh onto the filled gabions. I had obviously made a mistake in checking the stores when they were delivered, or else someone had walked off with two full rolls of wire. This seemed unlikely; the Afar, unlike some tribes I had worked with in other parts of Africa where theft was a sport and everything was at risk, don't make a habit of stealing. The shortage meant another trip to the town was necessary before we could complete the gabions in the dam wall.

Tefera's driver came up with another solution. He knew I needed to send some letters and Tefera would be wanting to know how things were going, so he could take the Land Rover to the town, post my mail, report to the governor and bring back more wire. Why hadn't I thought of that? It was a good suggestion.

So as not to hold things up while he was away, we got on with another important job, sealing the dam. The principle of a sand dam requires a watertight barrier; gabions are far from watertight. They are, however easy to install, slightly flexible and adaptable to unusual shapes and profiles. Waterproofing them is easily achieved by the use of a waterproof membrane on the upstream side. For this we were using neoprene sheeting which would be cemented into the rock of the river bed with waterproof cement.

Wire solution: the author (framed by a gabion) agrees to send Tefera's driver for more wire.

A large roll of neoprene had been delivered with the other supplies. Sand for making the cement was no problem as there was plenty in the river bed. We just needed to sieve it to get the right granular size. To make the cement waterproof I had bought a specialist branded product from a building materials supplier in Dessie. The rest was just hard work.

A line was marked out and a group of five men with hammers and chisels cut a groove into the rock across the river bed between the two rock outcrops, just upstream of the filled gabions. While they were doing that, others unrolled the neoprene and we cut it to fit so that the upper edge just overlapped the top of the gabions. When the groove was ready, the lower edge of the neoprene was inserted in the groove and cemented in, with flat rocks over the bottom to hold it in place. The rest of the sheet was draped over the back of the gabion wall and rocks were put along the top to hold it in position.

The wall itself was complete. The missing wire was required for lacing the last top flaps closed and for a flat mattress-like gabion to lean against the upstream face making a sandwich of the neoprene membrane and holding it firmly in place. The mattress layer would extend right across the river, covering the rock outcrops as well and was the last element before large rocks and sand was put in upstream. All the rock necessary to fill the mattress was ready in piles. Now all that was required was the wire for lacing everything together.

It was three days before Tefera's driver returned. When he did, he brought news of heavy rain in the mountains. We had estimated that it would take at least three days for the flow to get down to this point so, if any of it was coming down this channel, we would be tight for time to get everything finished.

So it proved to be. A small wave of water came down while we were still piling loose stone behind the dam. We had begun the back-filling further upstream some weeks earlier and this was the last section to be filled. Water began to accumulate and form a deep pond while we carried on throwing rocks into the gap. By the time we were done, the rocks were up to the level of the wall and extended back several hundred yards.

With only 185 men and women, we had moved nearly two thousand tons of rock in six and a half weeks. This meant each person had moved almost five hundred pounds of rock every day. It didn't seem possible, but the evidence was there, we had built a dam and backfilled behind it with rocks. Now all that remained was to cover the backfill with small stones and a twelve-inch layer of sand. There was a well near each bank from which the people could draw water, and drinking troughs for the livestock. We had built these using the last of the cement after sealing the membrane to the bedrock.

There would certainly be more rain coming down from the mountains this winter and from now on there would be a permanent watering hole here. Once the reservoir was full, any more water that came down would overflow the wall, cascade down a spillway and carry on downstream as it always had done.

This part of the drought relief programme at least had been achieved.

I GOT TO BATI A FEW days later to find Ato Abaye fuming about what I had done. He complained that he hadn't been properly consulted, the job hadn't been authorised and I had used materials allocated elsewhere.

"Which materials?" I asked.

"The gabions," he replied.

"And which project should they have been used for?"

He had no answer to this. I knew he wouldn't because until we started our mission he had never heard of a gabion and still didn't understand how they worked or what they could be used for.

When I asked why he had changed the original supply to the Weranzo site, he became evasive and changed the subject. Once again I found myself wondering why he was so keen for this programme to be a failure. It was a mystery, and so it remained.

ABOUT A WEEK BEFORE the sand dam was completed, we received a visit from a German medical team. The requirement for their services in the mountains had reduced enough for the *Bundesgrenzschutz* to keep their promise. From then onwards, they sent a team down to the desert every two weeks. They stopped at Eliwoha, then at Weranzo village and finally at the first worksite, which was now nearing completion under Mike's guidance. He got very friendly with one of the single nurses who made sure she was always included in the team that came down. Further encouragement came from a message I inscribed with gentian violet on his buttock. She saw it when she was asked to treat him for an inconvenient boil that had sprung up where he had got snagged by a thorn. She blushed most attractively when she read it and the rest, as they say, is history.

Our work was finished at the Chelaka dam and the majority of the people elected to move back nearer to Eliwoha. Most walked, following their few remaining animals, but Tefera's driver was helpful in returning with a truck to transport whatever baggage they wanted moved as, without camels, they would have been unable to do this themselves.

22 ~ A 'complication'

COMPLETING THE CHELAKA sand dam demonstrated that the Afar could learn to work and were capable of adopting other activities for their livelihood. If they could do this, with a little support, they should also be capable of using and maintaining the Weranzo irrigation system. Work on this had been supplemented by some earth-moving equipment. While the weir and all the head works were completed by manual labour, the main channel had been mechanically dug and soil around the field basins was bulldozed to form bunds. These were simple earth embankments about eighteen inches high around rectangular fields. They were designed to hold the water in when it came down the channel so that it could soak into the fields. Agriculturalists from the commercial cotton plantation at Dubti were on standby to come and supervise the planting as soon as any water came down the dry wadis.

The Afar clans in the area had benefited significantly from the food-for-work programmes and from the extra relief the new District Governor had provided. They now had regular visits from the German medical team and their general health was much improved. The Germans, however, could stay only a few more months and the Ethiopian government had so far failed to come up with any plan for continuing the medical service for the Afar. It looked likely that it would cease altogether as soon as the expatriates went home.

Rain to the south in Somalia and Hararge had eased the burden on the Issa and their raids had ceased. I would like to say it was because of the action we took and the presence of Ethiopian soldiers on the frontier, but they had stayed only a few days, then packed up and returned to Dessie. The truth was the Issa no longer needed to raid as, with rain and improved pasture, their own herds were doing well enough to sustain them.

After the Chelaka dam was completed, I took all the sultan's rifles back to him. He seemed a little surprised as he had half expected the tribesmen who had used them to steal them. But I didn't give him back the ammunition. This was shared out among the Abu Sama'ara men who were able to strut around posing with full bandoliers even if the rounds they carried were the wrong calibre for the rifles they possessed. Vanity is a wonderful thing.

BACK IN THE MOUNTAINS, the delivery of the *Blue Peter* oxen had to be overseen to make sure that all the animals arrived in good condition. They were supposed to have been inspected by a vet where they were purchased, but there was some doubt about this. One of the animals in the truck which arrived at the drop-off point was definitely sick. It was not acceptable for all the money collected by children in the UK to support this project to be wasted for lack of a simple veterinary check, so I asked Ato Yusuf Medellin, the LMB veterinary assistant in the area, to come and have another look them. He rejected five of the beasts, which threw the people organising the shipment into a real tizzy as they would have to find replacements in time for the film crew to record the delivery. They were once again on site and keen to get on with their job. The hauliers started arguing and protesting that we could walk these animals to the village and make the delivery for the film crew and then bring in replacements later. This sounded like the thin end of a wedge. Ato Yusuf saw straight through the ruse. Once some animals had been delivered, the sick ones would never be replaced if we allowed this.

After an hour of arguing, we seemed to be getting nowhere. Yusuf was getting fed up so he made a decision. He would not allow sick animals to be delivered to a clean area and risk spreading disease. He went to his car, returned a few moments later with a pistol and shot all five of the sick oxen.

This caused uproar among the transporters who immediately claimed compensation for their animals and demanded to be paid again, in advance, for going to find replacements. Yusuf ignored them, brought out a report book and began filling in forms. He wrote a separate report for each animal, detailing what was wrong with it and then issued two more forms to the delivery men. They looked at these with horror as they amounted to legal charges against the men for moving sick livestock and spreading disease. Under the drought regulations still in force, this was a particularly serious offence carrying a mandatory five-year prison sentence. He offered the men thirty-six hours to bring five healthy oxen; otherwise he would enforce the charges. So saying, he slapped handcuffs on one of the delivery men and chained him to the bumper of his car. The man would remain there until the others came back with the new oxen.

They looked very upset. I wondered if they would bother

Ato Yusuf took no nonsense over the oxen.

bringing more oxen. Maybe they would just take the money they had been paid and run. As they climbed into their lorry and drove off, I asked Yusuf how sure he was that they would ever return.

"Oh, they'll come back," Yusuf laughed. "This man is their father. He's well known to the LMB."

The drovers returned the following afternoon with five healthy oxen. The delivery was made, the film crew recorded the oxen being driven along narrow mountain paths, their arrival in the village and the first ox being hitched up to a plough and put to work. They filmed the animals drinking at the water troughs we had built along the route and corralled in new holding pens at the village. And they filmed a ceremony in the village and the villagers' joy at being pulled back from the brink after the devastation of the drought.

Two days later the film crew went home. When I returned to

the UK myself, I spent two days sitting with Biddy Baxter in the BBC editing suite, editing the film and writing a commentary for the programme. I was supposed to read the voice-over for this but the difference between the climate in the desert and London and the airconditioned environment of the studio gave me a sore throat and I lost my voice. In the end, somebody else did the job with a different script and using only a small part of the miles of film shot.

I went for a last visit to some of the relief operations that were still going. Most of the emergency was over and some of the camps' inhabitants had gone home. But more than twenty thousand refugees remained in the Bati camp. It would be more than a year before the last of them left.

AS FOR ALIAMU Hamid, in the end he had only stayed in the Bati camp for a few weeks. He told me he felt so lonely without his goats and his wives that one day he just walked out and headed homewards. It took him four days to walk back to Eliwoha. It was pure chance that I visited the village only a few hours after he arrived and heard of his return. I went to his *a'ari* and found him in much better spirits than the last time we had met.

His brother had looked after all his goats quite well and his wives were very pleased to see him. He looked well fed and his wound was very much improved. It was significantly smaller than when I had first seen it and his skin was growing back over the raw patches. But I was worried that if he discontinued the treatment it would get worse again.

After some discussion, he agreed that as long as he could remain with his family he would follow the same regime as he had been doing at the camp, provided I gave him the bowl and disinfectant. It was easy enough for me to purchase the supplies and also to get the same pills Dr Foster had been giving him. I bought a packet of envelopes and filled these with daily doses, leaving him one envelope for each day and replacing them once a week when I visited. To make sure he didn't give any of the pills to anyone else, I told him they were specific to his illness; if he gave any of them to his wives or to anyone else, it would make them sterile. He must have taken this seriously because he always had the right number of envelopes left when I saw him and his wound continued to improve. New skin, though tender and blotchy, grew back and restored his scrotum and his penis looked less like a gnawed dog chew.

Aliamu had been home seven weeks when I made my last visit to him and he proudly announced that his youngest wife was now pregnant. This news made all the effort, and the arguments I had had with Aliamu, entirely worthwhile. Thank God I hadn't let the doctor use his scalpel.

AT THE LAST RELIEF committee meeting I attended in Dessie, the Ethiopian government representatives were notable by their absence. It dismayed me that all the talk was still about relief. Even now, with the pressure off, none of the agencies had begun thinking about reconstruction or aid programmes to prevent a similar disaster occurring in a few years' time. All the evidence was that this situation would repeat itself, but nobody seemed concerned with doing anything to prevent it or to have programmes in place to reduce its effects. The accent was solely on relief in the present time frame.

This was not the first time drought had struck the region, although it had been spectacularly more severe on this occasion. Diminishing rainfall and famine were endemic in this part of the world and the way the weather cycles had been changing made it a certainty that in future years the rain would fail again. But nobody wanted to talk about that. They were mentally exhausted from dealing with this emergency. Their international sponsors wouldn't consider planning for another. However much I tried to get people to look to the future, nobody with any influence wanted to hear.

I wrote a long and detailed report and submitted it to London along with my project report. Even there nobody then or later was willing to give me more than a brief hearing. The director, while acknowledging that what I was saying was valid, was too tied up with other political priorities to put this on her agenda. HMG certainly didn't intend to commit themselves to providing any of that kind0 of aid; it simply didn't offer the right sort of political brownie points.

On top of that, the politics of Ethiopia were about to change dramatically.

I LEFT THE LAND ROVER at the LMB office in Dessie and took a bus back to Addis Ababa, departing at five-thirty in the morning. Overcrowded and top heavy with baggage piled on the roof, it cruised its way down the winding mountain road from Dessie to Kombolcha at what felt, from my position wedged between two well-wrapped women two-thirds of way back in the bus, like breakneck speed. It was a good thing we were travelling in darkness as the view out of the window was alarming.

The cramped environment of the overloaded bus was very sociable and despite speaking no Amharic, I got along well enough with my fellow passengers. We had all come prepared with baskets of food for the journey. Bits of fruit, little grilled liver kebabs and other things passed between fellow travellers. One enterprising woman even brought a Primus stove which she set up in the gangway and made coffee. How she managed to avoid setting fire to her own clothing and that of the people sitting close by remains a mystery, but her coffee was most welcome and she charged a fair price.

This bus went only as far as Kombolcha. Those of us going on to Addis Ababa boarded another one that was going all the way. When this one stopped in Debre Berhan, I made a final visit to the café where we had stopped so often in the early days of the mission. The owner filled my food pannier with fresh *injera* and *wat* to sustain me through my onward journey. Half an hour later, the bus pulled out, heading onwards across the plateau.

Travelling by bus gave me an opportunity to observe the countryside in a way that had been impossible while driving. It was interesting to see how carefully the fields had been terraced onto the mountain sides, with long, narrow strips following the contours like curving steps up the steep incline. Farmers were ploughing with simple peg ploughs, pulled by a single ox or sometimes a pair, making long sinewy furrows in terrain where it was impossible to see more than a few yards ahead before the field curved out of sight. The ends of each furrow might be half a mile apart along the hillside and yet only a few yards away across a steep ravine or round the other side of a shoulder.

My neighbour on the second bus spoke English and told me that in good years the farmers would get two crops of barley or *teff* off these fields. There was relatively little variation in the seasons up here and, being in the mountains, there was normally less difference between wet and dry seasons. When the rain failed, however, it was bad, because the soil was free draining and didn't retain enough moisture to sustain the crop for more than a week or two without needing to be watered again. I was surprised not to see water storage tanks all over the place; fewer than ten were visible from the road on the whole journey.

BACK IN ADDIS ABABA, I attended a series of meetings between the international agencies participating in the relief effort, most of which had been in Wollo Province. They put a lot of effort into reviewing what had been done and evaluating its effectiveness, but again I was dismayed that almost nobody was prepared to discuss ongoing programmes to prevent a similar situation occurring again. Even some members of the Ethiopian government with whom I raised this subject seemed blasé about the future. No matter how much evidence was offered about climate cycles, rainfall data and accounts from the people who lived in the desert, nobody wanted to listen. They maintained their work had shown that the world community cared, dealt with this drought and saved a few lives, and that was what mattered. Never mind about the hundreds of thousands of children who had been saved this time but would certainly be starving again before they became teenagers.

THE DEVELOPMENT ATTACHÉ at the embassy didn't want to talk to me; she was still smarting over the fact that the director had been out to visit and she'd not been involved. It mattered not that I had also invited her on three occasions to leave her embassy office and come down to the desert to see what we were doing; she had always found reasons why she couldn't come. I was now marked *persona non grata* in her book and the rest of the diplomatic crowd were equally stuffy and unhelpful.

My final meetings at the LMB offices were inconclusive. I left detailed information about the support that would be needed by the Afar with suggestions about how this could best be supplied and funded. Several of the senior executives listened politely but I felt they were just going through the motions. An unspoken undercurrent made it clear that the Danakil was not destined to get any support. There were other concerns afoot which were far more important to them. Unfortunately nobody was willing to say what these were.

Tefera hinted at the nature of these concerns over dinner one evening. He had come to the capital on official business. He told me about disquiet in certain quarters and his fears that something was about to erupt. His loyalty to the Emperor was still unshaken but he was concerned that Haile Selassie, who was now a very old man, had become an easy target to young firebrands who were beginning to become politically active. The Crown Prince was no help, being a sickly man who spent much of his time in a Swiss sanatorium. The empire was at risk and this worried Tefera.

Despite all this gloomy talk, we had a good evening together. He thanked me for the work I had done among the Afar and assured me that as long as he was the District Governor in Bati, they would continue to be supported.

As a direct result of what had been achieved in the desert, a second development project with the Afar had been proposed for World Bank support. I had been told the Ethiopians wanted me to return and lead part of the programme in the southern Danakil and the Ministry of Agriculture, under whose auspices the proposal had been made, wanted to talk to me about it before I went home. I had enjoyed working with the Afar and was certainly willing to do so again.

On my final morning, therefore, I went to the ministry for a meeting. A lot more thought had been put into planning this new programme than had been the case with our mission and it had a number of good components. It also sought to extend agriculture into more of the Awash valley by taking advantage of the commercial support available from the Mitchell Cotts agricultural team already working in Dubti.

The meeting droned on and finally broke up at about three o'clock. I would only just have time to get out to the airport and catch my flight home. As I was leaving, the Minister of Agriculture took me aside for a last word. He thanked me for my contribution and then told me that I would not be invited back with the World Bank project, even if it did go ahead, which he thought unlikely.

"Why is that?" I asked.

"It is because you would be a risk to us down in the desert," he said.

"A risk? In what way?"

"We have all read *The Seven Pillars of Wisdom* and we don't want you raising another army among the Afar. That would complicate things when the revolution starts."

"Revolution?"

"Yes, they are going to arrest the Emperor tomorrow morning. Now, go home and thank you."

I BROODED ALL THE WAY to London about what I had been told. When the plane landed in the small hours the following morning, I rushed to the nearest telephone and called the duty officer at the Foreign Office to let them know what was going on. The man on duty didn't take my call seriously and when I asked to speak to his superior bluntly told me to get lost and stop wasting his time. It was clear I wasn't getting through.

So I rang Anna Greening, the lady who had sent me to Ethiopia in the first place. Before leaving the desert she had given me her home phone number. She was surprised to hear from me, but listened carefully then told me to go and get some breakfast in the arrivals hall and wait to be collected. She would wake someone up and make them listen.

Forty minutes later, her driver arrived and led me out to the Daimler parked outside. In the back I found the director and a very senior colleague from the Foreign Office, together with the nameless man who had ridden with us when I departed for Ethiopia. During the drive into London, I explained everything I had learned. Once in an office, a debriefing team took over and asked me questions for two hours until we were interrupted by a messenger telling us the government broadcast monitoring service had just picked up news of a coup in Addis Ababa. Emperor Haile Selassie had been arrested and many of his ministers and officials had been shot.

23 ~ Dirty money well spent

FOUR YEARS LATER, HAVING had enough of government schemes, politics and bureaucracy, I was working in the Arabian Gulf as managing director of a high-tech irrigation company, Al Jouf-Reed. My Danakil days were a fading memory when out of the blue a telex arrived from a colleague at our sister company in Jordan asking for assistance. A shipment of irrigation equipment on its way from an Australian factory to Jordan had been lost en route. His enquiries to date suggested that it might have been transhipped in Djibouti, but it had never reached its destination in Aqaba. Since I was familiar with that territory, was there any chance that I could find out what had happened to it?

I sent a few telexes to people I knew in Djibouti, but without a lot of hope. A week later, I had all their replies. No one could find any sign of the shipment. Wondering how hard they had tried and suspecting not very, I decided to go and have a look for myself. So I booked a flight to Sana'a and onward to Aden. From there I caught a coastal steamer and two days later landed in Djibouti.

The place looked just the same as the last time I had been here, near the end of my stay in Ethiopia. The same immigration officers were at the port and the same customs officers still lounged indolently in their shed, a ramshackle apology for a building at the end of the main quay.

It didn't take long to find the shipping office but, being a Thursday afternoon, it was already closed for the weekend. Nobody would be there until Saturday. I tried a few other offices where I might pick up a lead, but made little progress. People were going home. I wandered through the docks, idly looking at piles of cargo stacked and waiting for collection, shipment by train to Ethiopia, or onward despatch by some other transport.

A pale grey stack caught my eye. I walked over to have a closer look. It was a stack of four-inch, B-class plastic irrigation pipe, made in the Iplex factory in Australia. There was no destination label visible, but then it was standing close to a container and I could see only one side and one end of the stack. A bit further along the quay were five more stacks of similar pipe and two sealed shipping containers which looked as if they had come from the same source. The destination label was visible on one of these; it was clearly addressed to the company in Jordan. It looked like I had found the pipe.

I went back to my hotel and sent a telex to Jordan, copied to Australia, telling them I believed I had found their pipe and asking what the value was. The Jordan office had already closed for the weekend but the Australians were awake and responded in double quick time. They told me it was none of my business what the shipment was worth, all they required was a certificate from the shipping agents to state that it had been destroyed and could not be delivered. Once I had got that and sent it to them by courier I was to get out of there and go back to my own company in the Gulf.

This seemed a bit odd to me as there was clearly nothing

wrong with the pipe I had inspected. It ought to be recovered and sent on – unless someone was running a fiddle, that is. I decided to wait until Saturday morning and see what Jordan said. It was their pipe, after all.

BEING BACK IN DJIBOUTI was a treat because there were Afar people here and it gave me a chance to go and speak their language again and maybe pick up a little news about how things had been in the Danakil since my departure and after the revolution. I wasn't expecting great news, but perhaps there might be someone who had heard something; the desert was normally so quick to pass on news, despite its apparent emptiness.

I found a small group of Afar men the following afternoon. To my delight, one of them knew who I was when I told him my name. We had never met, but he had heard about me and knew men who had been involved with both the Weranzo and the Chelaka schemes. We sat and drank endless cups of thick coffee and talked about places and people we knew until the sun went down.

On Saturday morning, I went in search of the shipping agent. He was profusely apologetic about the muddle with the cargo, which had happened because the ship on which it was supposed to be carried up the Red Sea to Aqaba had been too small and couldn't take all of the cargo waiting for it. It was due to come back to collect the pipe and the two containers but had since developed engine trouble. It would be out of service for at least three months.

"Couldn't the pipe have gone on another vessel?" I asked.

The agent looked blank. There was only this one ship plying the route between Djibouti and Aqaba. It would have to wait.

"But if that plastic is left out in the sun, it will degrade," I explained. He shrugged. It was not his problem if people didn't pack their goods properly for shipment. *Insh'allah*, delays happened and that's the way it was.

My enquiry about a certificate to say that the cargo had been accidentally destroyed or damaged beyond use was met with a gesture of rubbing his thumb across the tips of his finger as he held his hand out towards me. It was clear that he expected to be paid for this and the level of destruction certified would depend on the extent of my generosity.

"How much?" I asked.

He shrugged his shoulders, unwilling to commit himself precisely. "It is not easy, this," he said.

What the hell, I thought, it's not my money and it's going to be claimed from the insurance; the Australians will just add what I give him to what they claim, so why worry? I dropped 250 US dollars on the table and it vanished in the blink of an eye. I added two more hundred dollar bills and suggested I could write the words for him and then he would ensure that the customs officers released the cargo. The man eyes shone bright with delight as these notes also vanished.

AN HOUR LATER I HAD the certificate of destruction and a clearance certificate from the customs officer. This meant I could remove the pipe and the containers of tubing from the docks whenever I liked. Provided it was all shifted within twenty-one days, there would be no demurrage charges. I returned to my hotel and sent a telex telling the Australians I had their certificate and asking what I should do with the cargo.

Do what the heck you like, just lose it permanently, came the reply. It was like offering a bag of sweets to a child.

I thought over lunch about what to do with the cargo. In the afternoon, I made some phone calls and sent a few telexes to irrigation people I knew in the region. By supper time I had sold the whole lot for ten thousand US dollars to a Yemeni, the money to be paid in cash the following morning.

I walked down to the market area and found two Afar men, told them the name of the man I had met the previous day and said I would like to talk to him again. I also wanted to talk to anyone from the Dodha or Abu Sama'ara tribes who might be in town and I would return to the market in the middle of the morning tomorrow.

That evening I borrowed a typewriter from the office in the hotel and set about creating a diversionary paper trail so that the sale of the pipes and tubing could not be traced back either to me, my company, or to the Australian or Jordanian companies. By bed time I had also prepared a bill of sale, ready to give to my purchaser, always supposing he turned up with the cash in the morning. As a last shot, I sent a telex to my own office to say that I was taking a few days' annual leave and would not be back in the office until the following week.

I went to bed that night pleased with my day's work and slept well in the airconditioned comfort of the Hotel de la Liberté. It wouldn't be as comfortable for the next week; I would be on the ground, out in the desert.

NEXT MORNING THE Yemeni was as good as his word and turned up promptly with a bundle of cash. The deal was done and the cargo now belonged to him.

As soon as he left me, I headed for the market to see if my Afar friend had got the message. Not only he, but tribesmen who had worked on the Weranzo site and knew me well were there waiting. Before the morning was over, three more people I knew had joined us and we had a merry reunion. They told me a lot about what had happened in the desert after I had left and what conditions were like now. Tefera had kept his promise and continued to channel food and support to the desert for as long as he remained governor. Sadly this was only a short period because less than three months after the revolution, he was arrested and shot for being a supporter of the Emperor. Another man with strong communist ideals and no love for the Afar was installed in his place. The supply of food soon dried up, but not before the new commissar had been down to the desert to see if there was any profit he could accrue from the irrigation site.

If he had gone three weeks earlier he might have been in luck, but the cotton crop had already been harvested and sold. The money it raised had been distributed among all those who had worked on building the irrigation system. Under the new regime, none of the Afar felt disposed to work on it the following season, although the mountain monsoon still came down the *wadi* and the weir diverted some water into the channel and partially flooded the fields. But almost no crops were planted and the system was left unused and forlorn. The goats and sheep, however, did well because water being trapped in the field basins encouraged grass to grow and the grazing had been good for the last two years.

Talking to these men and hearing all this news served to strengthen my desire to go back there myself. I spent the following morning buying things from wholesalers in Djibouti while my new friends gathered a herd of transport camels. They brought fifty-four beasts when we met again on the third day. I had a huge pile of goods to transport; bulk items ranging from sugar and milk powder to cooking pots, enamel bowls of various sizes, kitchen knives, blankets, bales of cotton cloth, sewing needles and thread, rope, plastic sheeting and a host of other things that would be useful. After buying all this I had used more of the money to buy three thousand silver Maria Theresa dollars.

In the quiet of the late evening, we loaded the camels and slipped out of town, travelling through the night to get as far from the city as possible before anyone with a mind to interfere realised where we had gone. The next day, after resting through the morning, we crossed the frontier during the hottest part of the day, while any frontier guards there might have been were dozing, and headed west.

When travelling, the Afar do not appear to hurry but can keep a steady pace for long periods; it is surprising how rapidly the miles disappear behind them. We carried jerry cans with plenty of water so had little need to stop except for a five-hour rest and food at sunset. We walked steadily for eighteen hours each day and two and a half days later reached Weranzo.

Word that we were coming had gone ahead and there were nearly three hundred people waiting to meet us. One of the first I met was Farasabba Mohamed, who was now by far the oldest man in the tribe. He was thin and tired, but his eyes were bright and he gripped my arm with a claw-like hand as if he didn't want to let go. Others I knew arrived and many more whose names I could not remember but who remembered me. I looked around, hoping to see a few people who had become special friends, but there were gaps.

Doga Detolali was still alive but he was away in Bati and, although word had been sent to summon him home, he didn't arrive while I was there.

Ali Waré during the project's life.

Ali Waré, the trouble-maker who became one of my most trusted friends, was not there either. Shortly before I had left the Danakil, he had told me it was he who shot my mule and who threw the spear which stuck in my leg. Now he was missing, killed the previous year in a dispute with a man from the Asa'imara tribe over one of his wives. I wondered if he would still be alive if he'd had his *gillé*; he'd given it to me when I was leaving, as a gift by which to remember him – I have it to this day – but I was assured this would have made no difference. The Asa'imara man had shot him with his Kalashnikov, a weapon which, after the revolution, became increasingly commonplace and cheap. I saw that many of the men now toted these weapons although they still had their old bandoliers filled with ancient ammunition.

Once the camels had been unloaded, I asked Farasabba and the other *dagnyas* to organise the distribution of the goods we had brought. They sensibly put some of each item aside for people who were not there and wrapped the lot in one of the plastic sheets. After all the food, goods and chattels had been shared out, all that was left was the sack of silver coins. They asked me how these should be distributed and I suggested we should take a lesson from the day Ali Waré had caused the fight. They should tip all the coins in a heap, then each person would come and take one. If there were enough they would come and take another and so on until they were all gone. The discussion about this lasted an hour, but there were people present who had been there on the day I was talking about. They spoke up, saying this was a fair system. They knew I had never cheated them and always respected their ways. The coins were a gift and it was rude to argue over gifts. They knew Ali Waré had been my friend and said he too would have respected this.

This last bit surprised me but it was nice to know that my friend's memory still held the respect of so many in the tribe. It made his demise all the more poignant.

So that's what we did. A few coins were put aside for absent friends and then everyone took a coin, starting with the youngest. When I suggested the distribution should include Fred, who still ran his bar by the roadside, there was a lot of laughter but no one disagreed and he too took his turn. In the end everyone got at least four coins and the few that remained were added to the pile for those not present. Everyone was happy. We had had a good party.

It had been an entirely Afar affair as the police post was no longer occupied. The police had disappeared soon after the Emperor was arrested. Trucks and tankers still carried fuel and goods up the road from Assab to Bati but it seemed a lot of other things had changed since the revolution. And yet these people seemed the same.

I slept in the open that night and the following morning a crowd of us walked to look at the irrigation site. It was a sorry place, obviously neglected, but I was pleased to see that a few acres had still been cultivated, and were ready for planting when the water came again. A small group of hardy stalwarts, men who had become involved when I was first showing them how to grow tomatoes and spinach, were still working. I was not surprised to hear that Farasabba's sons were the leaders. He had been my first convert. With them were two other men, Ahmid Emaani and Digé Afwana, who had worked with the project from the beginning when we started making handles for the tools. They told me that others came and went and there would be more when the water came and it was time to plant the crop. I asked what they were growing and was told that most of it was down to tomatoes and a little corn. They had planted cotton the first year because the seed was given by the people at Dubti, but nobody could eat that so now they just grew food. I asked about growing crops as grazing and was amazed that although some of the unused basins had produced good grass, nobody had thought of cultivating this. I was disappointed that the Dubti team hadn't suggested it.

There was still a little money left in my 'pipe fund', so I promised to buy some alfalfa seed and send it to them. With a little work to repair the channels and maintain the field bunds, there was no reason why they should not be able to grow ten acres or more of good grazing. All it needed was seed and water to flow. The weir, for all it needed a little repair, still functioned.

The visit was all too brief. On that second afternoon, I and my companions from Djibouti began the long walk back to the coast. With the camels unloaded we moved faster on the return journey. Once more we crossed the frontier during the heat of the day and came back to the city by a southerly route, the camels peeling off with their owners in ones and twos so that our group shrank the closer we got to the market place. If anyone asked where we had been, we could say we had gone out into the desert locally for a few days to talk about old times. In the event, nobody asked.

Even after ordering the alfalfa seed and paying for it to be delivered, a small amount of money remained from my sale of the 'destroyed' cargo. So I took this to an orphanage in Djibouti and gave them a donation to buy new clothes and mosquito nets for the children in their charge. It may have been dirty money, but at least this way it would be put towards something worthwhile.

The following day I caught a boat to Aden and an onward flight to Muscat where one of the engineers from my company picked me up and took me back to our office in neighbouring UAE.

THE WERANZO RIVER has changed its direction over the last three decades. The river channel no longer brings water to the weir, which has been all but obliterated by successive floods re-sculpting the land. The irrigation system is barely visible now and the fields have fallen into disuse. Rain has fallen only briefly and on rare occasions since we were there.

While the principle of using the monsoon runoff was demonstrated, the effort required to keep it going was more than the Afar could manage unaided. Without ongoing support, irrigated cultivation has proved not to be viable as an alternative means of livelihood for the people living in that region. It could, however, be done again and if it was done a slightly different way, the Afar could still become nomadic farmers, cultivating small plots for grazing and a little food in different locations each year.

The Chelaka sand dam still maintains a good reservoir, providing water even at the end of the driest season. It's not an obvious construction and the only people who now know exactly where it is are the Abu Sama'ara people of the Meklet clan.

Epilogue ~ The futility of relief

AFTER THE REVOLUTION, the World Bank project never did go ahead. The Afar were given no further help after the Danakil Irrigation Mission ended, their last lifeline from the Ethiopian government ending with the removal of District Governor Tefera. In London, the new administration elected in February 1974 wouldn't entertain requests for development funds for that area and disengaged completely from any future involvement. Politics was being played at a higher level and HMG's refusal to do business with the Derg, the new government in Addis Ababa, meant that no development assistance would be given to any part of Ethiopia for a long time.

Even today, after a so-called democratic government has replaced the Derg, the only aid given by Britain is the subject of savage criticism by the likes of Human Rights Watch and the BBC *Newsnight* programme. They maintain that assistance from the Department for International Development (DFID) is being politically controlled by factions in Ethiopia and that DFID has no field representation and little idea what is actually occurring on the ground.

One or two of the international charities still maintain a low-key presence in Ethiopia, but their primary concern is relief. They have never extended their work into development programmes aimed at preventing repetition of the problems which so dramatically filled the world's television screens in the early Seventies.

Back then, events moved on, disasters in other countries shifted the agencies' focus. The world forgot about all the poor people of Ethiopia and the Danakil.

When it happened again in 1985, there was a renewed outpouring of humanitarian concern, with new players entering the field to ensure that the rest of the world took notice and donated generously. Two pop stars, Bob Geldof and Midge Ure, mounted the famous Live Aid concert. It raised a reported total in excess of £100 million which was distributed by the Live Aid Trust. Geldof went on to promote activities designed to lessen the impact of future droughts, but few listened.

The world's press behaved in its usual fickle fashion. After a few weeks of sensational headlines and photos of starving children, the media circus moved on. This happened in both the 1973-4 and the 1985 droughts. Most of the good work went unreported because good news doesn't sell newspapers or return the viewing figures that allow media moguls to charge advertisers top rates.

On top of that, the public gets weary of disasters. Initially we're horrified, revolted, thrilled and enthralled by it, and respond by digging deep. But our compassion soon wears thin; people become blasé. In a few short weeks, only a very few stalwarts even continue to care. The public's charity gets overdrawn and the tap runs dry in more ways than one.

This short-term attitude may be understandable, given the vast number of demands for charitable support that, week by week, are laid before the donating public. But it does not absolve those in a position to influence events, the world's governments, from the responsibilities they so adroitly dodge. The developed nations dole out aid, much of it wrapped up in long-term loan agreements, and thereby perpetuate the problems.

This is highlighted by one of Africa's brightest economic stars, Dambissa Moyo, a Zambian-born graduate of Oxford University and the Harvard Business School who for eight years worked in the World Bank before moving to Goldman Sachs. Her book *Dead Aid* exposes the sham and the failings of the aid system, warts and all. Corruption, she writes, is at an all-time high and any political influence the donor countries hoped to achieve through their aid is a mere illusion. Their efforts to use aid to promote a western style of democracy have come to nothing since the aid merely maintains the tyrants who have been bought off by it.

IN THE 1970S, THE problems to a large degree resulting from the drought in Ethiopia, and certainly most of the drama that was used to rouse public support, grew out of the huge numbers of very young children involved. It is the same in Somalia today. They were, and still are, only there in such numbers because infant mortality is so high. It's a vicious circle. Parents feel they must have large families in the hope that one or two of their offspring might survive to adulthood and be able to care for them in their old age.

Old age is perhaps a misleading term. Current UNICEF figures put life expectancy for most Ethiopians at only fifty-six, and in the areas regularly affected by drought, much less.

This attitude toward breeding is endemic throughout Africa and in the poorest countries of Asia. In many parts of Africa, almost fifty per cent of children die before they reach the age of two. The imperative to have replacements is therefore very strong. Even if they survive infancy, twenty-one per cent of children will die before they reach five or six and only in the most prosperous families will any of the remainder reach their teenage years with a chance to live out a full life.

Blaine Harden, sub-Saharan bureau chief for the *Washington Post* from 1985 to 1989, observed in his book *Africa – Dispatches from a Fragile Continent* that "Africa is the most successful producer of babies in the world and the world's least successful producer of food." While this is true right across the continent, its effects are all the more marked in the areas where drought is more frequent. This includes the countries that make up the Sahel and all those in the Horn of Africa, where drought has struck again today, affecting even larger numbers than before.

Besides the cultural imperative, the causes of high infant mortality include childhood diseases, malnutrition and lack of basic hygiene. Add to this the burden of too many mouths to feed, the declining yield of traditional crops under adverse climatic conditions and the fact that in sparse years families have to eat their seed grain just to survive the winter. With less seed to plant, the next harvest will be reduced. And so continues a downward spiral which can only end in another famine, unless the cycle is broken by external intervention.

Relief alone is not enough to do this; it just keeps alive a lot of people who would otherwise have died, to starve next year.

To make matters worse, climate change has resulted in a major expansion of the areas traditionally affected by low rainfall. Drought is now the expectation rather than the exception.

Science offers some hope. However much some people may

disagree with genetic modification (GM), studies show it can improve the drought tolerance and yields or food crops which may help prevent famine. However, the science remains unproven. Experts at the Commonwealth Scientific and Industrial Research Organisation (CSIRO), Australia's national science agency, predict it may take thirty years for the benefits seen in field trials to reach places that need them the most.

Even if the science does eventually work out, the great global combines that control the GM seed banks will be looking for a return on their substantial investment in research. They are businessmen, not benefactors. So, unless rich governments buy this seed and donate it to farmers in countries like Ethiopia, Somalia, Sudan, Kenya or across the Sahel, it won't help those who desperately need it. They will continue to live precariously .

It is no wonder so many people from the affected countries want to migrate to Europe to escape the inevitable.

GOVERNMENTS SEEM TO like channelling their aid through large prestigious projects and tying it all up with complex loan and trade agreements. My experience tells me that, sadly, any benefits that the aid brings to the most needy are secondary to obtaining and maintaining political influence. Programmes may be presented as having significant economic benefits for recipient countries, but they are usually riddled with inappropriate conditions. In my experience, few among their populations actually benefit. In addition, operating aid programmes through local government bodies leaves the finances of these projects open to leaching by middlemen. Little of the money given in this way actually goes any further than people in the local hierarchy who use it to make themselves richer.

But aid programmes look good at home, once the spin doctors get to work. The incongruity in 2012 of the UK donating millions of pounds to India when the Indians are themselves investing in nuclear weapons, space satellites and vast international steel empires is easily distracted. Politicians point to the extreme poverty in rural India, showing that they support initiatives aimed at relieving it. And of course there is a large bloc of voters in the UK of Indian descent. So the anachronism continues.

AT ECONOMIC SUMMIT meetings, the leaders of the world's most prosperous nations make great promises, pledging to do something about relief of the poor countries' debts. But delivering on their promises is another matter. When challenged, they offer excuses: the government changed and the incoming administration is not bound by their predecessors' commitments. Or they are still working on how best to do it without destabilising the recipient governments.

This is all flim-flam. Those who made such promises probably never had any real intention of keeping them. Even when Bob Geldof (now Sir Bob) challenged the world leaders at the G8 summit in Gleneagles, Scotland, and they reiterated their grand promises, almost nothing was done to relieve Third World debts. So the poorest countries in the world remain hamstrung by overbearing debt and, even if their political situations did offer the opportunity and the will to do so, they are ill-equipped to do much for themselves.

It is left to few non-governmental organisations (NGOs) and charities to mount small schemes and programmes in isolated places, just to show that someone cares and has not forgotten: charities such as Water Aid, Oxfam, Save the Children and others.

But their programmes are chronically under-funded. They are also subject to changing local political whims that make any worthwhile work extremely difficult and ensure that the results remain strictly localised. The local fat cats even manage to take the cream off these charitable programmes as the cycle of corruption and self-interest perpetuates itself.

The NGO programmes almost invariably shy away from doing anything to educate people about having fewer children and being more effective parents. Sometimes this inertia comes from obsessive attention to political correctness, fear of contradicting the indigenous culture and the claim that it is a basic human right to have children. The overpopulation is exacerbated by the endemic lack of basic health care and the drift from the countryside to the cities, concentrating people in huge slum areas where it is next to impossible to carry out any effective development or educational work.

TO MAKE THINGS WORSE, at the beginning of the twenty-first century we now have politics, piracy and fundamental religion getting in the way. Back in the 1970s, although there was a political undercurrent in Ethiopia, the drought was not exacerbated by politics of this sort. It was not the revolution that drove people from their farms and villages to seek help, but simple hunger and thirst caused by a natural calamity. Politics remained at an elite level. When it came, the revolution didn't initially affect the majority of the population. Only later did new rules impinge on their lives; for many, it was the same old domination and deprivation they had always suffered, but under a different banner.

In Somalia today, civil war has been raging between opposing warlords for almost ten years. It makes the effects of the drought so much worse as the population flees in terror. Since relief can't come to them, and they are not safe where they are, they go elsewhere in search of it.

In September 2011, with the rains due, we saw people who had fled to the towns in search of aid being forced to return to their villages by warlords who gave them only a month's supply of food. They could till the soil but it would be a year before any crop was produced. Meanwhile they were dependent on promises of aid which might never reach them.

The fact that in many areas Somalis were already migrating from their traditional territories because of failed harvests seems somewhat irrelevant when politics multiplies the movement. It still imposes an impossible burden on neighbouring Kenya, making the work of the relief agencies all but impossible.

During the Ethiopian drought in the Seventies, the total number of people affected was calculated to be about two million. Ten years later, when Geldof started Live Aid, the numbers had more than doubled and the geographical area affected was five times bigger. Today the numbers are larger still; official figures quoted by the BBC put the number of people affected at more than twelve million, the majority of them under ten years old.

Drought and famine will certainly return to the region in a few years time. Unless something is done now to ease the burden it will impose and to make the people more able to cope, the next time will be even worse. I wouldn't go as far as the great satirist Jonathan Swift who, in his *Modest Proposal* of 1729, suggested that the Irish poor should eat their excess children as a means of surviving the potato famine, and he of course was using a scandalous suggestion to highlight the true scandal of the situation. But effective birth control and education about how to keep one or two children healthy and surviving could have great value. It would, of course, require significant cultural change, but if those worst affected are not prepared to make some adaptation, why should the rest of the world keep coming to their rescue? This is an issue the African governments must address. Only they can take the necessary steps to manage their populations in proportion to what the land can support. And they must.

It is easy to make the excuse that cultural change is unrealistic, but that is not true where there is the political will and the necessary support. Everyone said the Afar could never change their habits and be brought to work, but they did.

I know; I was there.

And with a little help and encouragement they would do it again. Yes, it was often a frustrating process and it took a long time to achieve only a little. But we demonstrated most emphatically that it can be done. What we did at the Chelaka River could be repeated in many other places in that desert. Water from small sand dam reservoirs could as easily be used for small-scale food production as for watering rapacious livestock and, with ongoing education and the right motivation, eventually a compromise between goat herding and cultivation would emerge.

By the same token, long-term programmes to limit the number of births and to educate the population in hygiene, basic nutrition and resource management are a necessary component of cultural change initiatives. The aid to make them effective could be tied up with contractual obligations on the recipient government to support and participate actively.

Those governments in turn need to be motivated by real relief from the burdens that currently stop them doing anything. In most cases, this means cancellation of their nation's debts – that's what Sir Bob Geldof has been going on about for years. It is what Tony Blair said he would do at the G8 summit in 2000 and then whinged about five years later when he had failed to deliver on his promise. As no government since then has made any move to rescind that debt, the strangling yoke remains in place.

REMOVAL OF THE DEBT burden is only a small part of the recipe. Africa's countries need to stand on their own feet. Instead of aid, we should be working towards making African states economically viable and attractive to commercial investment.

Times are changing. The new foreign presence in Africa comes from the East. The Chinese are quietly extending their influence and investing in Africa. Their economy is booming and they need Africa's resources. Journalists and other observers tell us the Chinese make sure that the local people get a good return for their involvement. They have the sense to take a long-term view and invest in infrastructure. In forty years it may turn out to be another form of colonialism but does that really matter if their client countries have by then emerged from poverty?

Investment is not the whole answer, but it is a necessary part of it. Nevertheless there are other factors that keep Africa poor. One thing that outsiders invariably fail to recognise, or to take account of if they do know about it, is the effect of the extended family system on African economics. The extended family has so many ramifications of obligation and responsibility, usually extending outwards through the most tenuous relationships which allow the many to impose a parasitic drain far more voracious than anything occurring elsewhere in the natural world.

While it means everybody gets a small share of any riches, it also spreads the gain so thinly that it is next to valueless and unable to fuel real progress. It is barely enough for sustenance.

The system is the cause of so many unnecessary jobs being created through nepotism that businesses and bureaucracies become overloaded with non-effective people. It drains the resources of anyone who manages to make any small gain through their own efforts, with the result that their only recourse to stay ahead of the game is to become ever more greedy in the knowledge that whatever they get will have to be shared with legions. As much as the international aid system, the African extended family is part of the problem. This is another aspect of culture than needs to change, but it will take generations.

THEN WE COME TO the vexed issue of corruption, what it is and what it isn't. Western minds have a problem accepting that when a deal is made in Africa, everyone involved needs to feel they have benefited if the deal is to work. What westerners often call corruption is, in my experience, nothing more than the African way of doing business; middlemen are an accepted part of the process. Bilateral aid programmes routinely have a portion of their budget allocated to paying for 'incentives'. The new and draconian UK Bribery Act supposedly does away with that – at whose cost ultimately?

In reality, I expect another mechanism will be devised so these payments can continue. It's easier to play the game you know than to rewrite the rules and retrain the players, risking losing any political influence, or at least the illusion of it, that the current system has achieved. The sad truth is that corruption doesn't only exist among those in power in certain African countries.

There is no doubt, however, that corruption easily creeps in when the deal is not transparent. This is one of the major problems with the way aid has been given over the last fifty years. It is also why dictators have remained in place and democracy has never really taken root in Africa. Rwanda's President, Paul Kagame, interviewed in *Time* magazine in 2007, said more than $300 billion had been spent in Africa since the Second World War on "creating and supporting client regimes of one type or another, with minimal regard to developmental outcomes." Many of these regimes, as history shows us, were venal and corrupt in the extreme, one of the most prominent examples being Mobutu's kleptocracy in Zaïre which was financed by the CIA as part of the Cold War effort to limit the Soviet Union's influence in central and southern Africa.

What is wrong with being open about who gains from the deal? Granted, it becomes a little more complicated when dealing with a government like Mobutu's, but he was using the same principle; he motivated people by making them feel they had gained even if his penalties for failure were harsh. But then he was a dictator and made no pretence of democracy.

Western donors seem obsessed with their own concept of what democracy should be without understanding that it may not suit and may not be what Africa wants. It goes so much against traditional cultures. It may be better to leave Africans to sort out their own politics without interference. Only then might they find a system that allows them to create the conditions that will attract genuine long-term investors and allow their economies to develop. Then they can take responsibility for dealing with their own droughts and famines.

To make development effective what is needed is firstly wholesale cancellation of all sovereign debts resulting from development initiatives or political alliances. After that, any development aid that is given needs to be strongly conditional. Money should only be paid after the developmental conditions have been met, with the payments being made to the people who actually did the work and require the aid, not to government fat cats. Furthermore, it must all be done with absolute transparency. By doing this openly, making sure that people can see how everyone, including themselves, has benefited, corruption can be stopped, a lot more real development can be achieved, and the programmes stand some chance of gaining popular support.

Programmes must address the fundamental issues and problems which drag the relief agencies and the giving public into the arena every time there is a natural disaster. They need to use resources on the basis of what is needed, not what is desirable or because it looks good to the voters.

This is particularly true in the case of water, where rationing is an essential part of responsible exploitation. The indiscriminate sinking of large, deep boreholes and the ensuing production of hundreds of thousands of gallons per day is pure folly. The aquifers tapped will quickly be depleted; rainfall cannot replenish them as quickly as man can pump them dry. And when there is no more water, what then? More emergency aid?

The need for relief could be hugely reduced if something was done now. But warm words are just so much hot air. More promises of sovereign debt relief were made, at the urging of Bill Gates, during the sixth G20 Cannes summit in October 2011. But attention was soon diverted to the euro crisis and the prospect of action slid to a very distant back burner.

Sadly, good ideas, however valid they may be, stand little chance against the vested interests of donor democracies. Until somebody actually turns off the aid tap and changes the status quo, things will carry on as they are and Africa will slip further down the poverty scale. World Bank, IMF and governmental figures show that $2 trillion of aid money has been pumped into Africa over the last fifty years and yet all but two of Africa's nations are poorer today than they were fifty years ago. Because of the way aid is given, the slide into deeper poverty is already happening: the UN Human Development Report of 2007 predicted that fully one-third of the world's poverty will be located in sub-Saharan Africa by 2015.

IN REALITY, I EXPECT THE world will carry on as it does now. Rich nations will continue looking after their own, writing off colossal amounts of national debt when it suits them. But if they can do that for Greece when it is faced with an economic crisis, why is nothing being done to cancel the debts crippling the poorest countries in the developing world which face infinitely worse humanitarian crises?

At the same time, it is notable that almost no aid for the victims of the current drought in Somalia and Kenya has come from any African nation. As I write this, the Tunis-based African Union has offered $300 million over five years for famine relief, but this has only been backed by pledges of $57 million by African governments. In January 2012, the news services reported that less than $75,000 has actually been handed over and the probability is that the rest will never be paid.

Some African countries could afford to contribute, but they don't see it as their responsibility. At least they don't hold the poorer countries in debt the way the rich nations do.

It's a hard world and it needs tough action to reduce the future effects of drought and famine. I fear that for political attachments and emotional reasons, the rich countries will never do what is necessary. Our politicians just don't have the nerve to do anything that a few do-gooders among the voters might find unpalatable.

So the cycle will continue; drought and famine will return. In a few years our television screens and newspaper front pages will be filled again with skeletal, starving infants and queues of desperate people, and the numbers will again be bigger than before. Once again we will all dip into our pockets and later grumble about the necessity for doing so. Even then some of us will know that we could have done something to prevent such disaster. We could change the culture and reduce the effects, but our voices, even loud and well-known ones like Sir Bob's, will still be crying in the wilderness.

Glossary

aban – guide, safe conduct guarantor

amolé – salt

balabat – government appointed headman

dagnya – Afar elder

das – a horseshoe shaped grave monument. Plural: *wadella*

ga'abi – cotton cloak

makaban – traditional headman and leader.

mus'shäl – women's head covering

nasrani – non-Muslim; non-believer

sana'afil – skirt or kilt

Tribulus – short-lived ground cover plant with primrose yellow flowers and caltrop shaped thorny seeds. Probably *Tribulus terrestris*

wadi – dry riverbed, often subject to violent seasonal floods

Acknowledgements

EVENTS LIKE DROUGHT and famine stretch human endurance, patience and tolerance to their limits. On occasions this can lead to the breakdown of some of the manmade barriers of custom and tradition. Even so, despite the extreme situation, the acceptance of strangers living and working in their midst represented a major cultural shift for many of the Afar. I am grateful to all of those I encountered for their hospitality, co-operation and, in many cases, real friendship. It was my experience that the Afar people's hostile reputation was undeserved. I learned many things by being among them and am much the richer for the experience.

Many people contribute to a book, often in unseen and unexpected ways. So it is with this book. Getting shot in 1974 had unexpected consequences some years later and resulted directly in my becoming diabetic. This in turn, after many more years, resulted in my kidneys failing and in 2000 I was lucky enough to receive a cadaveric kidney transplant. I am eternally grateful to my donor and her family. Without their wonderful gift and the renewed life it gave me, I might not have lived to write this or my other books.

While I was writing the manuscript, many people both in UK and in Ethiopia gave me invaluable assistance by reminding me of events, people, situations and details and by checking records that were otherwise unavailable. Some of them are still in service but prefer to remain anonymous; nevertheless they deserve my thanks for their advice and assistance.

Once again my thanks go to Jenny and Alan Brand for intensive copy reading and for telling me when my words didn't make sense. Also for pointing out my bad typing when the spell checker in my computer could not cope with it.

I would like to express my sincere gratitude and admiration to Gary Henderson of GH Graphic Design Ltd for the series of very creative and original cover designs which have adorned my African Memoir series. His skill in weaving images together to highlight aspects of the stories within is original and most effective.

The most difficult task has again fallen to my editor, Chuck Grieve of Mosaïque Press, to whom I owe sincere thanks for his endless hard work, constructive criticism and infinite patience. He makes editing and the preproduction phases of bringing a book to publication an enjoyable and developmental experience and this deserves full recognition. My thanks to him also for the many cups of excellent coffee which lubricate our working meetings.

Finally I must thank my lovely wife, Gay, for her patience while I was writing, checking and proofing. Also for her supportive nagging whenever I am in danger of overdoing it without resting brain or body. Without her care and support neither this, not any of my other books, would have been completed.

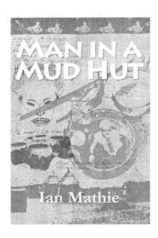

A compelling true story of water wells, Whitehall,
corruption, witchcraft and murder – steeped in the
redeeming qualities of humanity and the rich tribal
culture of West Africa. *Man in a Mud Hut* is Ian Mathie
at his finest as an observer, informed companion of the
armchair traveller and raconteur.

"An intriguing book... which will have you turning pages in
excitement and curiosity." – CULTURALLY BOUND

"Absolutely terrific... Ian Mathie deserves a wider audience. His
writing is spare, uncomplicated and unassuming... but quietly tells
an authentic and powerful story." – THE BOOKBAG

"If you appreciate page-turning story-telling, readability and
simplicity... being overwhelmed when you least expect it... being
educated as well as entertained in the real rather than the
imaginary world – then read this book." – AMAZON

"An entertaining book... fascinating tale." – DUTCHNEWS

West Africa in the 1970s: a volatile *mélange* of old and new; of aspiration, corruption, power and influence. Circumstances contrived to place Ian Mathie in the company of four heads of state whose rule had immense impact, positive and negative, on their countries and on West and Central Africa.

"Deliciously written, at times laugh-out-loud funny."
– WENDY REISS, author and editor

"Scores of fascinating adventures, projects, characters and extraordinary meetings in colonial Africa... amazing accounts of life in the forests." – BANBURY GUARDIAN

"Ian Mathie knows exactly how to stitch up a good story... simply the best of the relatively unknown writers." – THE BOOKBAG

IAN MATHIE'S BOOKS ARE AVAILABLE FROM MOST BOOKSHOPS, ONLINE RETAILERS OR DIRECT FROM THE PUBLISHER AT WWW.MOSAIQUEPRESS.CO.UK

Lightning Source UK Ltd.
Milton Keynes UK
UKOW031048070312

188466UK00002B/2/P